WINNING COMPANIES; WINNING PEOPLE

WINNING COMPANIES;
WINNING PEOPLE

THE DIFFERING APPROACHES OF WINNERS AND LOSERS

Colin Coulson-Thomas

Kingsham
www.akdpress.com

First published in 2007
by Kingsham Press

Oldbury Complex
Marsh Lane
Easthampnett
Chichester, West Sussex
PO18 0JW
United Kingdom

Typeset in TimesTen

Printed and bound in the UK

ISBN: 1-904235-58-1

British Library Cataloging in Publication Data
A catalogue record of this book is available from the British Library

Coulson-Thomas, Colin

CONTENTS

OTHER BOOKS BY
PROFESSOR COLIN COULSON-THOMAS

'Creating the Global Company, successful internationalisation' (McGraw-Hill, 1992)

'Transforming the Company, bridging the gap between management myth and corporate reality' (Kogan Page, 1992)

'Creating Excellence in the Boardroom, A guide to shaping directorial competence and board effectiveness' (McGraw-Hill, 1993)

'Developing Directors, building an effective boardroom team' (McGraw-Hill, 1993)

'Business Process Re-engineering, Myth & Reality' (Kogan Page, 1994 & 1996)

'The Responsive Organisation, re-engineering new patterns of work' (Policy Publications, 1995)

'The Future of the Organization, achieving excellence through business transformation' (Kogan Page, 1997 & 1998)

'Developing a Corporate Learning Strategy, the key knowledge management challenge for the HR function' (Policy Publications, 1999).

'Individuals and Enterprise, creating entrepreneurs for the new millennium through personal transformation' (Blackhall Publishing, 1999)

'The Information Entrepreneur, changing requirements for corporate and individual success' (3Com Active Business Unit, 2000)

'Shaping Things to Come, strategies for creating alternative enterprises' (Blackhall Publishing, 2001)

'Pricing for Profit, the critical success factors' (Policy Publications, 2002)

'Transforming the Company, manage change, compete and win' (Kogan Page, 2002 & 2004)

'The Knowledge Entrepreneur' (Kogan Page, 2003)

[Joint] 'Winning New Business, the critical success factors' (Policy Publications, 2003)

[Forthcoming new editions] 'Creating Excellence in the Boardroom' and 'Developing Directors' (Kogan Page)

All of these publications can be ordered from the bookshop of the networking firm: www.ntwkfirm.com/bookshop

ABOUT THE AUTHOR

PROFESSOR COLIN COULSON-THOMAS

MSc (Econ), MSc, MA, AM, MPA, DPA, PhD, FCA, FCCA,
FCIS, FMS, FCMI, FCIPR, FCIPD

Prof Colin J Coulson-Thomas helps boards and entrepreneurial teams to create and exploit knowledge, differentiate their offerings and develop their businesses. He leads the winning business research and best practice programme – the largest of its type in the world – and has reviewed the processes and practices for winning business of over 100 companies. An authority on director and board development he counsels individual directors and entrepreneurs and has advised over 100 boards on improving board and/or corporate performance. A Senior Academic at the University of Lincoln in the UK he is a regular speaker at corporate events and international conferences. He has given some 300 presentations in over 20 countries.

An experienced businessman Colin is currently Chairman of Adaptation Ltd; Cotoco Ltd and Policy Publications Ltd. Until recently Head of the Centre for Competitiveness and a Professor of Competitiveness (University of Luton), he is now Professor of Direction and Leadership at the University of Lincoln. A counsellor on business development and on corporate direction, transformation and learning, he helps boards to improve board and corporate performance. He is also Chairman of the Judges for the *e*-Business Innovations awards and a member of the Institute of Director's Professional Accreditation Committee and Board of Examiners.

Colin was appointed a Visiting Professor at the Management Development Institute, Delhi in 1997. From 1994–97 he was the Willmott Dixon Professor of Corporate Transformation, Dean of the Faculty of Management and Head of Putteridge Bury at the University of Luton and a Senior Associate at the Judge Institute of Cambridge

University. He was Hooker Distinguished Visiting Professor, McMaster University, Canada in 1995; and Visiting Professor, East China University of Science & Technology, Shanghai in 1996.

Formerly chairman of ASK Europe plc for eight years, he served for ten years on the Board of Moorfields Eye Hospital, and for six years as Deputy Chairman of the London Electricity Consultative Council. He served two terms on the Council for Professions Supplementary to Medicine, nine years on the National Biological Standards Board, five years on the Council of the Foundation for Science and Technology and four years as Corporate Affairs Adviser to the British Institute of Management. He is a past Chairman of the Crossbencher parliamentary liaison programme, a past Chairman and past President of the Focus Group, and was a member of the European Commission's Team Europe.

Colin has served on various corporate boards and governing bodies of representative, professional, learned, and voluntary institutes, societies and associations, including as chairman and president. He led the European Commission's COBRA initiative which examined restructuring across Europe, was the principal author and co-presenter of the 'employment and training' module of the 'CBI Initiative 1992', and is the principal author of the 'Induction Package for New TEC Directors'.

Colin has led various change management, re-engineering and transformation projects and surveys of entrepreneurial/boardroom issues, attitudes and practice for the Institute of Directors, Institute of Management, Institute of Personnel Management, Government Departments and the NHS. Practical lessons derived from these surveys and work with entrepreneurs and boards are summarised in: 'Individuals and Enterprise' (Blackhall Publishing, 1999) and 'Creating Excellence in the Boardroom'/'Developing Directors, Building an Effective Boardroom Team' (McGraw-Hill, 1993 and Kogan Page, 2007).

His recent publications include 'Creating the Global Company: Successful Internationalisation' (McGraw-Hill, 1992), 'Transforming the Company' (Kogan Page, 1992, revised edition 2002), 'The Future of the Organisation: Achieving Excellence through Business Transformation' (Kogan Page, 1997/8), 'Developing a Corporate Learning Strategy' (Policy Publications, 1999), 'Individuals and Enterprise' (Blackhall

Publishing, 1999), 'The Information Entrepreneur' (3Com, 2000), 'Shaping Things to Come' (Blackhall Publishing 2001), 'Pricing for Profit' (Policy Publications, 2002), and 'The Knowledge Entrepreneur' (Kogan Page, 2003). He is the editor of 'Business Process Re-engineering: Myth & Reality' (Kogan Page, 1994), and executive editor (all Policy Publications) of 'The Responsive Organisation: Re-engineering new patterns of work' (1995), 'The Competitive Network' (1996), 'Winning Major Bids' (1997), 'Developing Strategic Customers & Key Accounts' (1998), and the 'Winning new Business in ....' series of reports (1999–); and co-author of 'Winning New Business, the critical success factors' (Policy Publications, 2003).

Colin was educated at the London School of Economics (Trevennon Exhibitioner), London Business School, EAESP – Fundacao Getulio Vargas (Brasilian Government Scholar), and the Universities of Aston, Chicago (Deans List) and Southern California (Graduate School Distinction). He obtained first place prizes in the final examinations of three professions.

Contact address: Mill Reach, Mill Lane, Water Newton, Cambridgeshire, PE8 6LY, UK

Telephone: +44 (0) 1733 361149; Fax: +44 (0) 1733 361459; Email: colinct@tiscali.co.uk; www.coulson-thomas.com

ACKNOWLEDGEMENTS

I would like to thank my colleagues at Lincoln Business School, the University of Lincoln, Adaptation Ltd, Cotoco Ltd, Policy Publications Ltd and The Networking Firm. I owe a special debt of gratitude to Susan Honeyborne, my parents Elsie and Joseph Coulson Thomas, and to Yvette, Vivien and Trystan Coulson-Thomas, to whom this book is dedicated, for their understanding during the many hours I spent writing the various books and reports, the key findings of which are summarized in this book.

Colin Coulson-Thomas
February 2006

INTRODUCTION

The question of why some people and certain teams are better than others at particular activities is an intriguing one that has spurred a life long investigation into how best to transform individual and corporate performance. Early inter and cross company comparisons suggested that even quite successful organisations usually find it very difficult to be effective across all areas of corporate operation.

Specific research projects were initiated to identify critical success factors for particular activities that are critical to commercial success. These investigations have invariably revealed both a wide spectrum of attainment and considerable differences in the importance those surveyed attached to the factors whose significance were being assessed.

The roots of many – and in some investigations most – of the identified critical success factors appear to be attitudinal and behavioural. The approaches of people who are successful at the various activities that have been examined differ from those of people who struggle and under perform. Put simply, high achievers do things differently.

The findings are consistent across overlapping areas of activity, and their implications are exciting. Building critical success factors and the approaches of high performers into corporate processes and support tools can enable average performers to adopt the approaches of superstars and emulate their achievements. Within every organisation that has been examined there is considerable potential for performance improvement.

This book summarises what superstars do differently, and how others can be helped to adopt their winning ways. But first some background to the Winning Companies, Winning People Research Programme and subsequent dissemination, development and implementation work.

The research programme and the individual research studies have been led by the author. Their aim has been to improve the effectiveness and contribution of corporate leaders, key workgroups and professionals in many parts of the world in important areas such as managing change (including re-engineering and new ways of working), winning business, building relationships, creating and exploiting know-how, and providing corporate direction.

Some of the areas investigated could be said to be general such as 'communication' and the responsibility of many people, while others such as pricing and purchasing could be regarded as more specific and left to particular individuals or teams. They range from setting the strategic direction of an organisation to managing its performance (see diagram in chapter 1).

The origins of the research programme lay in work concerning professionalisation, corporate leadership and the differing effectiveness of individual directors and knowledge workers during the late 1970s, and the author's roles with a number of professional associations. Early outputs included guide books and the first of a number of management methodologies (for developing new products).

Subsequent participant observer roles with matched pairs of professional bodies formed the basis of a research design for doctoral research into the process of professionalisation and the relative standing of different groups of professionals. Certain occupational groups were found to be more successful than others at securing status and formal recognition.

Within different groups of knowledge workers skewed distribution curves of competence and achievement were also observed. Typically there would be a small number of high performers and a long tail of barely adequate accomplishment. Some organisations were noticeably better than others at identifying their superstars, but so often the most capable worked on similar tasks to those allocated to their less able colleagues. Little if any effort was made to identify and record what they did differently, or use their approaches to improve the performance of others.

The next phase of investigation, involving over 2,000 companies, was concerned largely with different aspects of how to transition to higher performing and more effective and flexible models of operation. A family of studies examined corporate structures and processes, the competence of directors and the effectiveness of boards.

Other areas examined by questionnaire surveys included 'communicating for change' and 'harnessing the potential of groups'. Some of the findings were counter intuitive and challenged prevailing views at the time. For example, the impact of certain types of communication was found to be inversely related to the amount of effort devoted to refining, polishing and packaging them, while many groups were so distracted by operating effectively as a team they would loose sight of their objectives and purpose.

The current phase of the research programme began with an interest in why some directors, boards and professionals are so much more successful than others at certain activities such as winning business, and continues with an ongoing investigation of critical success factors that has now also involved over 2,000 organisations and the development of tools for sharing best practice that are used by leading companies.

The approach adopted is to identify apparent success factors through desk research, visits to representative companies and/or expert consultation, followed by questionnaire surveys and follow-up interviews. Companies surveyed range from major corporations to smaller companies.

Survey questionnaires are sent to those who are directly involved in – and responsible for – the area being investigated. The aim has been to record the views of people who understand both the approaches adopted within their companies and the results achieved. Practitioners appear more prepared to reveal their performance and approaches in some areas than others. Thus while over 300 participated in one winning business study a related pricing survey secured 73 respondents.

Participating companies are ranked according to outcome measures and top and bottom quartiles of attainment (or those above and below an average or mid point in the range of achievements according to the sample size) compared to isolate critical success factors. In some areas outcomes were easier to assess than in others. Thus success at competitive bidding was measured in terms of the proportion of bids won. The top quartile superstars – only 4.1 % of the total – were those winning more than three out of four of the competitive bid races they entered.

In other areas multiple measures of outcomes – or benefits achieved – were used. For example in the study of how companies develop strategic customers and key accounts 16 possible benefit objectives were assessed on a score of 1 to 5 (from 5 for "very effective" to 1 for "not effective") to give a maximum score of 80 (16×5) and a minimum of 16

(16 × 1). Among the 194 companies surveyed the highest score was 77 and the lowest 29, a range of 49.

Both the most effective and the least effective companies were to be found right across the size spectrum of the companies participating in the survey. Roughly twice as many (67%) of the most effective companies win more than half of their business from strategic customers compared with the least effective (35%). The most effective (winners) considered nearly four times as many of a possible 14 reasons for developing strategic customers to be 'very important' as the least effective companies (losers).

To illustrate the number of different areas that can be impacted by adopting winning behaviours the possible benefits considered in the effective strategic customer and key account management study were:

- improving key customer satisfaction, retention and loyalty;
- enhancing a company's image;
- acquiring relevant knowledge and know-how;
- enhancing a company's role in its value chain;
- increasing both general and individual customer profitability;
- reducing sales and administration costs;
- generating growth;
- extending global reach;
- improving market share;
- creating new strategic customers from an existing customer base and gaining them from competitors;
- increasing sales of specific products and services;
- funding product development;
- creating entry barriers for competitors; and
- lowering a company's dependence on any individual customer.

Adopting winning behaviours across all the many activities examined offers the prospect of transforming corporate performance. As we will see in chapter 24 there are now practical and cost effective ways of enabling average achievers to raise their game by adopting the approaches of high achievers. Enormous improvements in productivity and performance have been achieved, while implementation and management of change type issues have been avoided by equipping people with tools that make it much easier for them to do their jobs.

Particular 'rules of the game' can sometimes apply in certain sectors even though sector variations might not be apparent in data collected. In the case of the winning business sector studies that have been undertaken panels of expert practitioners within the sectors concerned have been assembled to assess and comment upon the findings. Resulting research reports (see Appendices A and B) have contained a selection of their views.

Over 4,000 companies have participated in individual research projects that have been undertaken by the author within the 'winning companies, winning people' programme. The research and resulting publications, approaches and methodologies (see Appendices A and B) have concerned the leadership, management and implementation of corporate leadership, transformation and business development. Over a twenty year period the programme has evolved and developed across five overlapping and inter-related streams:

- Corporate communications, and particularly: communication with customers and prospects, communicating for change, and the communications activities of corporate leaders (both individual directors and boards).
- The development of more competent directors and effective boards, particularly in terms of leading corporate transformation, communicating with stakeholders, creating an enterprise culture and putting the critical success factors for competing and winning in place.
- The management of change, corporate transformation, and the improvement and re-engineering of processes, including those for entrepreneurship, winning business, building relationships and creating and exploiting know-how.
- The critical success factors for corporate success in areas such as managing change, winning business, building customer and stakeholder relationships, and creating and exploiting know-how.
- Knowledge creation and exploitation to generate incremental revenues, enhance shareholder value, raise workgroup productivity and improve corporate performance.

The research questions posed at each step have been informed by previous research findings. The adoption of a distinct directorial perspective has helped to ensure a degree of cohesion, cross-referencing and cumulative enrichment and refinement of understanding and the development of more holistic approaches, while the involvement of professional bodies has helped to ensure successive research surveys were focused on contemporary concerns.

Individual research projects have been assisted by a variety of organisations, including the Association of Consulting Engineers, Chartered Institute of Marketing, European Institute of Purchasing Managers, Institute of Directors, Institute of Management, Institute of Practitioners in Advertising and publications such as Financial Director and Marketing Business. Some of the early individual studies were also funded by Government departments.

Presentation and discussion meetings to explore the implications of findings have been held at various associations, institutes, universities and other locations in Europe, Africa, Asia, North and South America and the Middle East. Workshops (see Appendix C) based upon project findings have also been delivered in Europe, Asia, Africa, the Middle East and North and South America in countries as far apart as South Africa and Russia and Canada and Brazil.

The research programme continues. It has consciously targeted under-researched areas such as bidding, while more recent developments with pioneering companies include work on a new generation of knowledge-based job-support tools that are transforming the performance of workgroups in some of the areas that have been examined. The investigating team is keen to involve further companies in this work.

The surveys of directors and boards undertaken during the period 1998-91 highlighted the need for director development. The work done is this area is currently being updated with a view to producing book outputs that are more accessible to trainers, consultants and practicing directors.

Certain of the research databases covering activities such as winning new business, building customer relationships and purchasing have also been constructed to enable bespoke benchmarking reports to be prepared for those who complete a survey questionnaire. Reports* compare corporate approaches with those of average and high performing (e.g. top quartile) companies and indicate areas that need attention in order to match the achievements of the 'superstars'. Completed questionnaires refresh the database and facilitate the updating of reports.

Much of the work which has been done has had a European or international dimension. Most of the companies participating in the surveys operate internationally. Among participants in the purchasing survey companies from the UK, France and Germany were particularly well represented, but there was also significant participation from Benelux, Italian and Nordic companies.

The re-engineering methodology that formed the basis of the responsive organisation and competitive network approaches (see appendices A and B) covering the introduction of new ways of working while re-engineering and the re-engineering of supply chains respectively resulted from an EU funded element of the programme. This study – Constraints and Opportunities for Business Restructuring, an Analysis (COBRA) – was a pan-European investigation of re-engineering, teleworking and business restructuring led by the author.

The 'COBRA' approach to re-engineering and corporate transformation formed the basis of subsequent EU funded research projects (e.g. ABUITTS, HOCAPRIT, MARCHIVE, COCO), and a further wave of EU funded application projects. HOCAPRIT and COCO were concerned with healthcare processes and healthcare in EU regions respectively. MARCHIVE produced a methodology for re-engineering Government archiving processes.

The involvement of public sector organisations in certain of the EU projects – and indeed some voluntary organisations in the COBRA investigation – revealed that the identification of critical success factors and successful approaches and the development of support tools to transform the performance of average operators and knowledge workers can also occur in 'non-profit' arenas. Adopting a similar approach to that advocated in this book could well achieve significant improvements in public sector productivity.

The research programme also formed the basis of ABUITTS. This particular EU funded project led to four national initiatives (Greece, Italy, Portugal and Spain) involving *inter alia* a programme of workshops for the founders and general managers of high-tech companies.

Feedback from participants included a request for particular help with business development processes.

Winning new business, whether from prospects or securing additional orders from existing customers and cross selling to them, remains a top priority for companies surveyed as markets become more competitive and they respond to an Asian challenge. Work on developing support tools has focused upon helping those who are in direct contact with customers and prospects (see www.Cotoco.com). Early tools incorporating the principle of capturing and sharing critical success factors and winning approaches won awards at both national and international level.

A by-product of EU involvement in certain projects has been the wider dissemination of programme findings. The emphasis in research programme outputs has steadily shifted from articles to share research findings with academics and senior decision makers to their incorporation in practical approaches, methodologies and tools and helping practitioners to transform the prospects of their organisations.

Outputs from the programme to date include 21 books, 58 research reports, some 500 articles and a programme of Masterclasses and workshops (see Appendix C). Over 300 seminar and conference presentations have been given in over 20 countries, and over 40 radio and TV broadcasts have been used to disseminate findings of the research programme. This book endeavours to provide a concise overview of the differing approaches of high performing winners and low achieving losers.

While a summary can loose the detail of individual research reports, the principles set out in this book have been substantiated through a number of in-depth investigations involving particular companies. These have included the review and improvement or re-engineering of processes examined by the research programme, and in some cases the design of new processes for a greenfield situation or new joint venture.

Projects have been undertaken for companies ranging from entrepreneurial businesses to globally operating 'household name' corporations. Much of the work has involved the review of processes and practices for winning business and/or improving the effectiveness of boards and the performance of key directors and their teams. This activity has further underlined the untapped potential that waits to be released in both people and organisations.

Working with teams on different continents has also revealed how people in diverse situations and circumstances can benefit from the programme's findings. While local considerations may influence how an approach can be implemented in a particular context the requirements for success in international markets need to be addressed if a company is to compete and win.

Consultancy assignments have been undertaken for over 100 major organisations, including several Government Departments. If one includes smaller companies, over 100 private and public sector boards have been helped to improve board and/or corporate performance, and winning business reviews have been undertaken for over 100 companies. It is hoped that key lessons which have emerged will be summarised in future new editions of some of the research reports.

Further Information

*Benchmarking services based upon continuing use of research databases developed by individual research projects are available covering building customer relationships, purchasing and winning business for both commercial companies and the following professions: accountancy, advertising, engineering consultancy, law, management consultancy, marketing and PR consultancy and IT consultancy.

CHAPTER 1
SETTING THE SCENE

Have you ever wondered why some companies expand, while others that appear to be in a similar situation plateau and contract? Are there certain business and management practices that lead on the one hand to growth and development, and on the other hand to stagnation and decline? Do the most successful operators know things that others are not aware of? Do they adopt different approaches?

In many sectors of the economy, competing companies appear to be offering similar products and services, and using the same or equivalent technologies, processes and systems. They recruit similar people, often from the same universities and business schools, employ the services of the same or similar consultants, and they invariably fall for the same management fashions and fads. Yet over time some businesses prosper while others wither. Why is this? What do the leaders of successful companies – or winners – do differently from losers who struggle and fail?

There are various rules of conduct aimed at equipping individuals to lead a moral life and achieve success. 'Self help' books feature prominently on airport bookstands. But what about achieving success for one's corporate organization? Are there equivalent rules or principles that, if adopted, might increase the chances of commercial success?

The author's continuing research programme has been considering the questions just posed for over 20 years (see Introduction, page xv). It examines areas that are critical to competing and winning such as improving performance, managing change, competitive bidding, building customer relationships and creating and exploiting know-how. The purpose of this research is to determine what boards and management teams need to do – and also what they should not do – to lead, innovate, pioneer, discover, compete and win.

This book provides a brief overview of the major findings to date in areas critical to business success. It is intentionally concentrated. The

aim is to present a compendium of concise summaries of research findings into the differing approaches of successful and unsuccessful companies for students, directors, managers and entrepreneurs with
ambitions to build successful businesses and realize their full potential.

The author's intention is to provide an authoritative, positive, realistic and inspiring 'go for it' book for ambitious directors, managers, business school students, entrepreneurs, and all those who want to achieve
both commercial success and the personal fulfilment that comes from
competing and winning.

There is a long established success literature for individuals. Titles on
the bookstands mentioned above range from the thought-provoking
and profound to the simplistic and lightweight, but there are far fewer
accessible, holistic and research-based approaches based upon a comparison of what effective and ineffective corporate directors, managers
and entrepreneurs actually do. Many of the books that consist largely of
assertions, 'gut feel' and 'writing from the heart' fail to identify the
activities that actually make the difference between winning and losing.

The present book is based upon differences between the approaches
and conduct of winners and losers – or leaders and laggards – as
revealed by the above-mentioned research programme led by the
author. It contrasts and compares how those who are successful (winners) and those who struggle and fail (losers) actually set about important activities such as winning business, buying, building customer
relationships and creating and exploiting know-how.

The critical success factors that have been identified are set out in a
series of research reports (see Appendix B). The more recent reports
specifically relating to winning business are set out in Appendix A. The
attitudes and approaches underlying or associated with these critical
success factors are summarised in the following chapters of this book.
For those interested in applying key lessons of the research programme
within their own business, Appendix C gives details of various master-
class, seminar, presentation and workshop modules that are available
and from which bespoke sessions can be created.

This book aims to be accessible but balanced. The intention is to present research findings in an easily digested form for busy readers. Most
of the chapters contain comparisons of the differing approaches of winners and losers. These are intended to show people what to do and what

not to do to succeed in an area that is important for business success, for example building effective boards, winning new business, partnering or corporate learning.

The introduction (page xv) provides an overview of the authors research programme. A selection of the major published outputs is presented as Appendix B for those interested in learning more about what has been discovered. This book will synthesise the key lessons from this body of work into a comprehensive summary of winning and losing approaches to business development.

In total, over 4,000 companies and knowledge-based businesses (e.g. professional firms) have participated in research projects led by the author. In the last decade, each of the research projects has ranked the outcomes achieved by participants and compared the approaches of those who are in the top and bottom quartiles or above and below the average or mid-point in the range of achievement, depending upon the number of participants and statistical considerations for determining the reliability and validity of findings.

Figure 1 shows the main areas covered by the research programme, the items in italics being the names of some of the books and reports that summarise the findings in the fields concerned. Areas examined range from establishing the strategic direction of a company to managing performance. Outputs include methodologies for transforming performance, introducing new ways of working, re-engineering processes and re-engineering supply chain relationships using e-commerce technologies.

From time to time books and reports that have been published are updated as new findings are processed.

Significantly for the readership of this book, while there are sector specific issues to address in most business sectors, its core messages – and the main differences of attitude, approach and behaviour of winners and losers – have been found to apply independently of sector and company size. Encouragingly also are the findings that many of the critical success factors and winning approaches are independent of each other. Hence success – as one might expect from the research methodology – increases with the number of them that are put in place.

In the studies that have been undertaken typically only a quarter – or at most a third – of the businesses examined were either a 'winner' or a

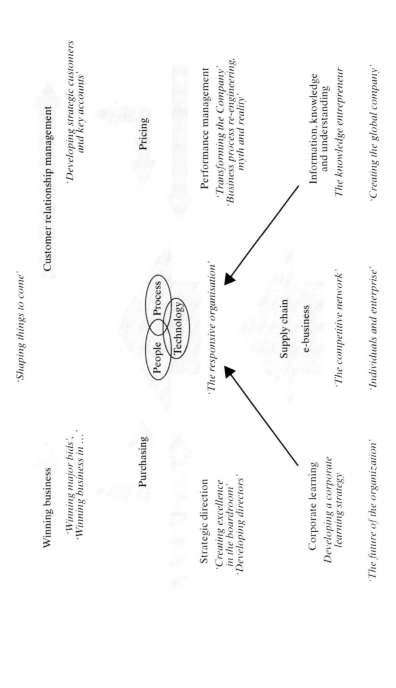

Figure 1 Colin Coulson-Thomas Research Programme ('*Transforming the Company*')

'leader'. Most of the teams examined were losers or laggards. Many well known or 'blue chip' companies are firmly in the loser or laggard category, despite considerable effort to improve their performance. Generally consulting and other activities to boost results missed the critical success factors in the areas concerned.

In most of the companies visited during the research, considerable resources were being devoted to areas that are not relevant to competing and winning. At the same time quick and easy ways of improving performance by simply putting the critical success factors in place and adopting winning approaches were ignored and overlooked. One can only speculate that losing behaviours and wasteful expenditures attract vested interests that benefit from their continuation.

Intriguingly, many well-known corporations that win in some areas are found to be losers in others. If this were not the case most of the world's output would be controlled by a handful of giant enterprises. However, many companies that appear well placed to prosper seem ignorant of the critical success factors identified in the research reports and remain unaware of whether or not they are adopting winning or losing approaches.

In some of the areas examined, even the most successful companies – those in the top quartile – are only very effective at less than a half of the critical success factors that have been identified. Hence, the research findings are very encouraging. There is enormous scope for improvement in all the businesses examined so far.

To date opportunities have been identified to improve the performance of every survey participant by introducing a change of attitude, behaviour or approach independent of systems and/or process changes. The lead-time for benefiting from improvements can be as short as the time taken to approach and undertake a particular activity in a winning way. Many people start behaving as winners from the moment a more successful approach is explained to them and understood.

The research programmes continue and winning approaches have been adopted and tested in many operational environments. They have also been embedded in tools and techniques described in chapter 24 of this book and in 'The Knowledge Entrepreneur' (Kogan Page, 2003).

The readership for whom the book is intended embraces company directors, managers in businesses of all sizes, consultants, professionals, business school students, entrepreneurs and business advisers who have had enough of retrenchment, downsizing, playing games, cosmetics, distractions, spin and management fads, and who want to get real and succeed through adopting positive, pro-active and evidence-based approaches.

One of the core themes of the book is that personal fulfilment and business success increasingly need to go hand in hand. Businesses can no longer sustain success at the expense of their people. It is therefore hoped that the book will be of much interest to individuals who wish to transform their prospects and quality of life, and become personally more successful, as well as those setting out to transform organizations and the fortunes of particular businesses.

The book is all about how to become a 'winner', someone who is both successful and fulfilled. It is intended to be honest rather than escapist. It endeavours to avoid peddling hyped concepts, panaceas or single solutions. Instead, it highlights the combination of elements and the attitudes, approaches and behaviours needed to succeed.

The book will show how companies can compete and win and how businesses can work with individuals to enable them to achieve both commercial success and personal fulfilment. While focusing on corporate governance, business development, personal success, management of change and entrepreneurship markets it also seeks to address contemporary work–life balance concerns.

Because it is research-based, the book will also hopefully ring true as an honest account of the differing attitudes and behaviours of winners and losers.

We live in a world of opportunities and problems that could be addressed by imaginative solutions. There is enormous scope for economic and social entrepreneurship. Success and failure are increasingly a matter of choice. Go for it.

CHAPTER 2

UNDERSTANDING THE BUSINESS AND MARKET ENVIRONMENT

The importance of strategic awareness and an understanding of the business and market environment within which companies operate was highlighted by an initial survey of 218 companies. Three quarters of the responses were from those holding the job titles of chairman or chairman and chief executive. Other surveys have examined certain issues or particular trends and developments in the business environment. For example, a survey of managing the relationship with the environment covered 104 organisations. Overwhelmingly, the responses were from those with environmental policy or implementation responsibility.

Some companies appear ambushed or taken by surprise by external events. They find themselves ill-prepared to react to both challenges and opportunities. Other businesses are much more alert to what is happening in the business and market environment in which they operate. They track issues, anticipate events and monitor competitive activities.

So what do the winners do differently in relation to understanding the business and market environment? To answer these questions research teams led by the author have examined the corporate experience of over 2,000 companies (see Introduction). The results are summarized in: 'Transforming the Company, Manage Change, Compete and Win' and the steps that boards can take to question and challenge prevailing assumptions are set out in 'Shaping Things to Come' a handbook for creating a better future*. In this chapter we look specifically at findings relating to understanding the business and market environment.

Let's start with unsuccessful boards or 'losers'. They are often unaware of impending challenges and pressing requirements to change.

They simply do not see them. They tend to be largely oblivious to developments in the market places in which they operate. They also do not anticipate or look ahead, and they are not alert to threats and opportunities. Hence, when they do wake up to what is at stake they may have little time in which to adapt even if they had the will and means of doing so.

Losers just hunker down. They make cosmetic references to environmental and social concerns in annual reports and accounts. They stick to what they know and feel comfortable with and plough ahead regardless, hoping any problems they encounter will blow over. If they do stop and take stock of where they are, it is generally infrequently. Whatever changes are made, tend to quickly become permanent features.

Opportunities can also be resisted if responding to them would require changed practices and behaviours. New requirements may be perceived as distractions until such times as they become so pressing and potentially lucrative that they can no longer be ignored or avoided. Some only act when legislators or competitive activity requires them to do so.

In contrast, the boards of successful companies or 'winners' have more acute and sensitive antennae. They look out for the weeds that can foul propellers. They are aware of what is happening around them and in the business and market environment. They are also entrepreneurial. They view problems as arenas of potential opportunity and take the initiative in shaping the future, challenging assumptions to create new options and choices.

Winners identify and monitor economic, political and technological trends, and assess their likely impacts upon both themselves and their customers. They then consider what, if anything, they should do in response. Such exercises are undertaken on a regular basis, and at least once a year. Resulting actions are subsequently reviewed and if need be challenged and amended as events unfold.

Because they read the road ahead, winners generally give themselves sufficient time to register, react and adapt. Changes are made quickly as and when they are needed. They are often implemented before they are imposed or otherwise formally required.

People in winning companies address problems rather than conceal, ignore or avoid them. Hence, they do not build up to a point at which they are either insurmountable or appear to be. Steps are taken one at a time. A series of adjustments over time – some small, others more fundamental – may allow winners to cope with radically altered circumstances.

Smart companies have an issue monitoring process (IMP) and undertake formal issue monitoring and management. If not undertaken more frequently this could be an annual exercise to which all board members, key personnel and even customers, suppliers and business partners might be asked to contribute. It should also precede any annual budgeting or planning.

IMP participants are asked to identify major issues, trends and developments in the external business environment, and consider: (i) how will they impact upon firstly the company and secondly its customers and suppliers; (ii) what the company needs to do in response at local, operating unit and group levels; and (iii) how it might be able to help customers and suppliers to respond (i.e. possible business opportunities).

Experienced users of IMP find that it is difficult to track more than ten issues at any one time, and better to concentrate effort on a smaller number of the more significant issues. To aid comprehension the summary of each issue, its impacts and what needs to be done in response should, ideally, be no more than a page. Those reporting issues should be asked to think through their implications and make practical recommendations for action to confront challenges and seize opportunities.

Significant positive developments and negative issues need to be continuously managed. If left unchecked even minority interests can grow like waterway weeds and block navigation. Proactive approaches can generate considerable goodwill. For example, BP-Amoco acknowledged the risks of global warming ahead of other oil companies and announced its intention of securing specific reductions in carbon dioxide emissions over a defined period.

Further Information

*'Transforming the Company, Manage Change, Compete and Win' (2002) by Colin Coulson-Thomas and published by Kogan Page.

'Shaping Things to Come, strategies for creating alternative enterprises' (2001) by Colin Coulson-Thomas and published by Blackhall Publishing.

CHAPTER 3

CREATING A
COMPELLING VISION

The need for a clear and compelling vision has emerged from several surveys within the winning companies, winning people research programme. Surveys of directors and boards, change managers and project managers have all highlighted the importance of visioning. Yet one survey within the programme involving over 60 entrepreneurs failed to uncover a single example of a vision that motivated people internally and focused their efforts or differentiated a company from its competitors. Visioning exercises have been undertaken for over 40 organisations.

Are your people, and those with whom you deal, clear about what your organisation is endeavouring to achieve? In this chapter we will examine what leaders of the most successful companies do differently when setting about the strategically important task of visioning.

A stretching, distinctive and compelling vision that paints a picture of a future, desired and attainable state of affairs can engage and motivate. A clear vision is of value internally and externally. Internally it motivates people to achieve and focus their efforts, while externally the vision should differentiate a company from its competitors.

The board is primarily responsible for formulating and agreeing a company's strategic vision and ensuring its implementation. In some companies particular individuals have been given the specific task of ensuring that a corporate vision remains current and vital. These keepers of the vision attract various job titles. At USA.net someone known as the Chief Visionary was appointed to undertake the role.

A vision should capture the essence of what a company is all about. At the start of the new millennium, Steve Ballmer became CEO of Microsoft. His predecessor Bill Gates, a co-founder of the company, assumed the title of chairman and chief software architect. The latter role allows Gates to return to his roots and the activities he most enjoys. It also reflects the importance of a strategic vision in the development of new technologies.

Some visions motivate more than others. Staff at the BBC became much more engaged when the public broadcaster's vision was changed from 'to be the best managed organisation in the public sector' and became 'to be the world's most creative organisation'. A vision and a mission statement should balance the needs of both individuals and the organisation along the lines of Amazon's 'Work Hard, Have Fun, Make History'.

Internally and externally, the common and shared element of a vision should be a unifying factor. It should hold a diverse, complex and network form of organisation together and provide its people with a sense of common purpose. Yet while a vision can inspire, it can also result in disillusionment and distrust if it is incomplete or incapable of achievement, and there is a gap between aspiration and attainment.

So what do the winners do differently in relation to visioning? To answer this question the research programme led by the author (see Introduction, page xv) has examined the corporate experience of over 2,000 companies. The results are summarized in: 'Transforming the Company, Manage Change, Compete and Win' and exercises that boards can undertake to develop new offerings and distinct strategies are set out in 'Shaping Things to Come'*. Winners and losers are distinguished by their visions.

The corporate visions of losers are often little more than words on paper. Most are instantly forgettable. A bland statement produced during an off-site 'planning day' is printed on a card and distributed to staff. Although it may make occasional appearances in corporate brochures, it is rarely referred to. Whatever 'visioning exercise' was undertaken is viewed as a one-off event. The outputs may linger on in unchanged form long after they have ceased to reflect what is possible, current or desirable.

Loser companies often lack a distinctive or compelling reason for existing. They are one of a kind or breed. They are not noticeably special or unique. People find it difficult to justify why they should join it, work with it, use its services or invest in it. Perhaps the initial underlying business concept lacked originality. Maybe it simply mirrored what competitors were already doing.

The wider world tends not to care when losers falter. External parties may have little interest in keeping such an enterprise alive. The corporate herd continues as individual stragglers fall by the wayside. Even failure may go largely unnoticed. While employees lose their jobs customers may be able to obtain very similar products and services from other suppliers.

Many of the key players within loser companies are uncertain and insecure. They lack self-confidence and have little self-esteem. Other people have little interest or faith in them. They themselves are not really sure what they are about. In difficult circumstances they may not have sufficient inner conviction or do enough to keep the enterprise alive. They throw in the towel and are relieved when shot of onerous responsibilities.

Losers can appear dull, resigned and subdued. They drift. They seem to lack drive, personality, heart and soul. Senior managers in corporate losers become preoccupied with 'fitting in', 'hanging onto customers', 'papering over cracks' and surviving. After a time they lose sight of corporate objectives and lose touch with past dreams and their inner selves.

In contrast, winners are confident, vibrant and driven. They fizz and are clear about what they are seeking to achieve. They are much more likely to have articulated a unique rationale. They endeavour to root their visions in real customer requirements. When it is described, people react. They usually understand it and they appreciate what is special about it.

Managers in winning companies feel important and wanted. They ensure that employees and business partners know what they have to do to bring a vision about. The vision lives and motivates because while it may be challenging it is also regarded as relevant and exciting. People are proud to be associated with it.

Winners stand out. They strive to be different. From the moment she first arrived in New York, Madonna endeavoured to meet the people who mattered. She registered and was remembered. Her single-minded determination to build her personal brand has made her a global icon. Richard Branson's ballooning exploits have helped to keep his name in front of the public and entrench his reputation as a business leader who is different from the traditional 'suit'.

Winning businesses connect. They also contribute. Their people try to make them special and unique. Customers may find it difficult to obtain similar goods and services elsewhere. They would certainly notice and be inconvenienced if the enterprise failed. Like investors they want it to do well.

When a winner stumbles, other people catch their breath. They are concerned. Because its role and contribution is important to them a variety of 'interested parties' including customers, suppliers and business partners might be willing to provide temporary support during difficult times. Because business fundamentals and the critical success factors for competitiveness are in place, investors may be willing to provide additional funding to allow a winning company to ride out an occasional storm.

Winners never rest on their laurels or become complacent. Their people are restless. They search, test, learn and apply. Directors of winning companies are much more likely to regularly review their vision, purpose, key corporate goals and strategies during board meetings to ensure they are still current and relevant. If they are found wanting, people throughout the organisation make whatever changes are necessary to reflect altered conditions and evolving requirements.

They are also much more confident, and less likely to 'cut and run' in crisis situations. Obstacles, difficulties and the unknown invariably confront those who venture ahead of the pack. People in winning companies derive self-worth and inner strength from the knowledge that their organisation is valued and needed. Senior managers do not need to play games or pretend to know things. They trust their instincts and are not afraid to be themselves.

External parties who deal with winners know where they stand with them. While they may be flexible and prepared to bend so far in the search for accommodation, they are unwilling to compromise cherished principles and core values. They also avoid promising more than they can deliver.

Winners are determined. Like a predator, they play to their strengths and can also be patient when waiting for the right moment to go after an opportunity. They acknowledge and confront challenges. In difficult times they are open and honest with those whose support they seek. They tell it as it is and share rather than conceal reality as they understand it. As a consequence, they are more likely to receive help when they ask for it.

Further Information

*'Transforming the Company, Manage Change, Compete and Win' (2002) by Colin Coulson-Thomas, published by Kogan Page.

'Shaping Things to Come, strategies for creating alternative enterprises' (2001) by Colin Coulson-Thomas, published by Blackhall Publishing.

CHAPTER 4

CREATING A WINNING BOARD

Initial investigations of director development and board operation and effectiveness involved 274 organisations. 247 of the survey responses were from chairmen or chief executives. Subsequent surveys have covered the development of IT and personnel directors, the role and development of particular categories of directors such as SME directors and NHS directors, and particular aspects of the work of directors and boards. Specific assignments have been undertaken for over 100 boards and mini surveys of communities of directors have been undertaken in a number of countries.

The boards of many companies axe jobs, cripple prospects and destroy shareholder wealth. Enron was advised by leading professionals, used fashionable approaches and invested in the latest technologies. Yet it all went wrong. What did the corporation's directors overlook? What do boards of successful companies do differently?

The leading performance improvement and transformation research programme led by the author (see Introduction, page xv) has examined why some companies grow while others stagnate. The experience of over 2,000 enterprises reveals that the prime responsibility for wide gaps between potential and achievement, and between intentions and outcomes, lies in the boardroom. In this chapter we consider the attitudes and approaches that distinguish between successful boards (winners) and unsuccessful boards (losers).

The essence of the difference in approach and behaviour between effective and ineffective boards, and the critical success factors for competing and winning that have been identified suggest that: (i) the corporate governance debate has done little to improve the contribution of many boards; and (ii) a different balance may need to be struck in many boardrooms*.

Corporate performance depends primarily upon what boards actually do and how their members behave. Winning boards are distinguished by the attitudes and conduct of their members. Corporate governance arrangements are often a symptom rather than a cause of board effectiveness.

The board should be the heart and soul of a company, the source of its ambition and drive. Whether or not a company competes and wins, sustains success and remains relevant usually depends upon its board. Without a sense of purpose, a sound strategy and the will to achieve, well endowed corporations wither and die.

Winning boards display the will to win and are driven to succeed. Their actions demonstrate they care. They understand what is happening in the business environment and marketplace. They anticipate events. They confront realities, take a longer-term view and provide strategic leadership.

Directors of winning boards assume personal and collective accountability for their actions. They understand the distinction between direction and management, and their directorial duties and responsibilities.

Winning boards concentrate upon the external, strategic and business development aspects of corporate governance. They strive to benefit shareholders by delivering additional value to customers. They provide and communicate clear direction, a distinctive vision, a compelling purpose, achievable goals and clear objectives.

Winners focus upon the critical success factors for competing and winning. They develop additional income streams, new capabilities and fresh intellectual capital. They invest in director development and the professional selection, appointment and induction of new directors. Their chairmen consciously build effective boards of competent directors.

In comparison, 'loser' boards lack will, drive and heart. Their members mouth generalizations and are easily distracted by pleasantries and trivia. They avoid responsibility and blame others for disappointing results. Their perspective is essentially defensive and short-term.

The directors of losing companies are preoccupied with their own status and remuneration. They confuse the roles of director, manager and shareholder. They concentrate upon internal, policing and steward-ship aspects of corporate governance, and engage in spin and damage limitation exercises to protect their reputations.

'Loser' directors confuse operational and strategic issues, and muddy personal and corporate interests. Many charming individuals who effortlessly assemble portfolios of independent directorships instinc-tively know when to look the other way and can be relied upon not to rock the boat. Insecure chief executives seek out their services.

Board members of loser companies fail to engage, excite or motivate people. They respond to developments rather than influence events. They focus almost exclusively upon financial measures of performance and the control of costs. They make little effort to review and improve their own effectiveness.

The boards of both winner and loser companies attract articulate and highly paid people. However, they distinguish themselves particularly in their respective approaches to managing change, leading transforma-tion and creating future opportunities.

Winning boards inspire, energise and motivate. They avoid rhetoric, blather and hype and address specific issues. They are determined, prag-matic and positive. They strive for success rather than survival. Instead of rationalizing disappointment, they learn from it.

Winners are also proactive. They approach those they would like to do business with. They set out to become business partners rather than commodity suppliers. They are also selective. They focus upon areas that make a difference. They understand that change can disrupt valued relationships, and only change what needs to be changed.

Winners support and enable the achievements of others. They trust reliable people and take calculated risks. They delegate and encourage entrepreneurship. In comparison, losers are self-interested and fear the unknown. They play it safe and avoid commitments.

'Losers' mouth platitudes, spread themselves thinly, and bark up the wrong trees. They also react, imitate and copy. They jump on bandwag-ons and adopt me-too approaches. They duck issues, fall for fads, embrace panaceas and search for single solutions.

Winners think for themselves and reflect before they act. They read the road ahead and assemble what they need to succeed. They adopt simple solutions and differentiate their companies' approaches, products and services. They shape the future by creating bespoke offerings, additional choices and new markets.

Finally, winning boards are self-aware. They monitor their own performance. They are open, welcome questions and invite feedback. They critique themselves and encourage challenge. They choose pragmatic colleagues and competent advisers.

Further Information

*New editions of 'Creating Excellence in the Boardroom' and 'Developing Directors' by Colin Coulson-Thomas are forthcoming and will be available from Kogan Page.

'Shaping Things to Come, strategies for creating alternative enterprises' (2001) by Colin Coulson-Thomas, published by Blackhall Publishing.

CHAPTER 5

CORPORATE GOVERNANCE

BOARDROOM QUESTIONS FOR CHALLENGING CONVENTIONAL WISDOM AND SHAPING THINGS TO COME

Aspects of the structure and accountability of boards have been examined in the course of a number of the surveys of directors and boards which have been undertaken within the winning companies, winning people research programme. One survey covering 60 boards was designed to secure the views of chairmen and chief executives of predominantly larger organisations, while another involving a similar number of companies has focused upon the governance of SMEs. Another exercise involving a programme of interviews led to a multimedia development package for a community of directors implementing certain government programmes. Good governance, directorial competences and board effectiveness were the main aims of the project.

Too many boardrooms are like chapels of rest, the only signs of life being the ticking of corporate governance checklists. A handbook for ambitious directors* written by the author argues that if boards are to add more value and create a better tomorrow, they must challenge conventional thinking and current practices. This chapter examines some further differences between successful and successful boards.

Many boards are failing to deliver. They are rubber stamping rather than shaping things to come, picking over the past rather than creating the future. Debates focus upon details and trappings within the rules of an existing game. Assumptions are not challenged. Efforts are not made to create a new game that might deliver more value to customers and shareholders and greater satisfaction to employees.

In a world of benchmarking and preoccupation with prevailing fashions and fads, certain behaviours, approaches and practices are assumed. People with similar backgrounds to their peers go with the flow. They look over their shoulders at others and imitate and copy them. They use the same or similar tools, techniques, systems and processes. Not surprisingly they come to similar conclusions as their competitors.

Different suppliers produce very similar offerings aimed at the same and largest customer segment their analyses identify, even though the many smaller segments of the market ignored might collectively constitute an overwhelming majority of people whose requirements could have been better addressed by alternatives. Cosy consensus, inertia and intellectual laziness prevent many companies from providing new and better options. Fundamental questions need to be asked in boardrooms.

A systematic investigation of the differing approaches of successful companies (winners) and their unsuccessful competitors (losers) has assembled sets of questions that directors can use to challenge prevailing assumptions and create new offerings that provide greater choice for consumers and communities.

The essence of good corporate governance is to achieve an appropriate balance between a number of critical factors, for example performance today and the capability to compete and win in the future. The investigation of how directors actually behave reveals that the practices and unchallenged assumptions of many boards are likely to condemn them to presiding over a losing company.

Striking a different balance, for example between activity and reflection or between action and reaction is often the key to greater boardroom effectiveness and marketplace success. Thus, whereas many losers appear to value activity for its own sake, reflection was much more evident among the members of successful boards. Often losers are so busy that they simply do not have time to think.

The concern of losers to be seen to be active and to be 'doing things' is evident in their approach to change. They exhibit an unquestioning and naïve faith in the benefits of change. Very often changes appear to be made for changes sake, for fear that a lack of restructuring or re-organisation might be taken as an indication that they are 'asleep on the job'.

Winners strive to achieve a balance between change and continuity. They recognize that while some change may be desirable, indeed inevitable, it can also be stressful and disruptive of valued relationships. Continuity is important in areas such as purpose and service. Customers who are unsure of what to expect may become unsettled, and they might take their custom elsewhere.

Looking at the balance different groups strike, for example between change and continuity or complexity and simplicity is also the key to creating new offerings. Thus many consumers – from members of re-enactment groups to purchasers of classic brands and houses with Georgian features in conservation villages – may favour continuity and might prefer aspects of the past. Others might desire products with fewer features that are easier to understand and use.

Losers are also more pre-occupied with reacting to the competitive moves of others, following fashions and jumping upon bandwagons. In comparison, winners are more likely to be proactive, for example when seeking ways of helping their customers and delivering more value to them. They take the initiative and approach prospects they would like to do business with, and work with them and business partners to explore new possibilities. They are not afraid to venture out in front, explore and discover.

Whereas losers are also pre-occupied with their own agendas and the achievement of corporate objectives, winners are more concerned with achieving a balance between individual and corporate interests. If changes have to be introduced they will strive to ensure they benefit the people concerned as well as help achieve corporate goals. They recognize that relationships which are mutually beneficial to all parties involved are more likely to last.

Directors, particularly independent directors, should question, probe and challenge. Is the right balance being struck in the above and other areas examined? Is there too much focus upon fads while insufficient attention is paid to the fundamentals – the core building blocks of corporate success, the critical success factors for competing and winning? Is the board addressing surface symptoms or the underlying substance?

Losing boards of struggling companies engage in spin to explain and rationalize events where winners would identify and address root causes. A balance has also to be achieved between packaging and assembling the elements that make up the package. Within the mix that makes some directors competent and certain boards effective, the willingness to pose critical questions that others overlook or are reluctant to ask can be a crucial ingredient.

To increase the likelihood of becoming a winning company, consciously build an effective board of competent and questioning directors. Avoid the distractions of trappings. Invest in director and board development. Be professional when selecting, appointing and inducting new directors. Go for those likely to rattle the cage.

Some individuals add value, others are parasitic or distractions. Aspiring winners should avoid the bloodsucker brigade and devious courtiers. Don't let your board become a form of outdoor relief for the semi-retired. Select practical and competent contributors. Find candidates who are quiet thinkers and will do what is right.

Further Information

'Shaping Things to Come, strategies for creating alternative enterprises' (2001) by Colin Coulson-Thomas, and published by Blackhall Publishing.

CHAPTER 6

DIFFERENTIATION

SHAPING THINGS TO COME:
STRATEGIES FOR CREATING
ALTERNATIVE ENTERPRISES

Differentiation has been considered in a number of studies within the winning companies, winning people research programme. It emerged as a significant factor – for the achievement of a price premium – in a survey of the pricing strategies, policies and tactics of 73 companies, and – for distinguishing a particular proposal – in the winning business surveys which have been undertaken covering over 300 companies and over 500 professional firms. Over 100 projects have been undertaken involving activities to differentiate an organisation's offerings from its competitors, while a survey of over 60 SMEs revealed a lack of differentiation as a common characteristic of the firms with falling turnover and profitability that were visited.

From time to time most boards are impatient for more sales. Directors grumble about the lack of interest shown by targeted prospects in corporate offerings, poor media coverage or disappointing reactions to presentations. But why should anyone be interested in their company's activities? What is distinctive about what they provide or do?

Research into the differing approaches of successful and unsuccessful companies (see Introduction, page xv) has resulted in guidance* for challenging cherished assumptions and creating new offerings that provide customers with additional choices. In this chapter we learn that businesses must be distinctive and differentiate their offerings to survive.

Many advertisements, mail shots, brochures and press releases fail to capture the attentions of their recipients or excite their imaginations.

We are interrupted by sales calls and inundated with junk mail. Proposals and prospectuses all seem the same. People sell to us rather than help us to buy by highlighting what is different about their offerings.

Consider your own company. Can you quickly communicate what it does? What is special or unique about its offerings? Do pitches for new business or requests for additional funding register and succeed? Do your colleagues' presentations bite? Does your corporate literature stand out? Is your presence noticed at exhibitions?

Does your company struggle to differentiate its offerings? If so, consider what the world would lose if it ceased to operate. What is different about its purpose, goals, values, brands, image and reputation? Does it offer new options and choices?

Above all, does your business supply its customers and offer its prospects, goods and services that they cannot get elsewhere. If your company were to close down, how much inconvenience would its customers really suffer? Could they obtain similar offerings from your competitors?

Many struggling enterprises or losers find it difficult to motivate their people, stand out and justify premium prices. They lack a compelling rationale and distinctive purpose. Their offerings and messages to the marketplace are largely indistinguishable from those of other suppliers. In short, many losers are bland, faceless or boring.

There is little excuse for this sorry state of affairs. There are countless possibilities for differentiation, and also endless opportunities for consumer, social and knowledge entrepreneurship. 'Me-too' approaches, copying and imitation lead to squeezed margins and consumer indifference. Increasingly, market leadership goes to those who create, pioneer and discover.

Although trading conditions may sometimes be tough, and competitive pressures can be severe, smart companies or winners balance cost-cutting with innovation. They break out of commodity product traps by differentiating their offerings. They deliver additional value to justify higher prices. They provide alternatives and address unmet needs.

Ambitious entrepreneurs do not wait for an economic upturn. Winners generate additional income streams by creating bespoke products for individual customers and establishing new markets. They bring their proposals and business plans alive with interesting angles, unusual approaches and novel offerings. They intrigue prospects, attract customers and secure venture capital or place new shares by being different.

Cautious suppliers play it safe. Losers tend to follow the herd. They seek refuge in large numbers and aim at the biggest market segments. They try not to make exceptions for particular customers in order to avoid 'systems problems' or increased transaction costs.

More courageous suppliers find that technological advances are making it easier to address individual needs. Mass customization is possible in ever more sectors. The Internet offers a cost-effective way of reaching scattered members of minority interests, people with common passions, shared obsessions and complementary aspirations. There may be enough of them to justify the creation of new and distinct offerings.

Increasingly, customers also like to stand out. More of them are demanding goods and services that reflect their individuality and personal requirements. They may be prepared to pay a higher price for customization through particular modifications, the addition of requested features or a more distinctive design.

Questions should be asked to determine whether the board of your company is adopting the losing approach of encouraging conformity and uniformity or behaving like the more successful winners and stimulating challenge and diversity. For example:

- How much emphasis is placed upon conforming to a corporate culture, exhibiting role model behaviour, benchmarking, competitor analysis and sharing received wisdom?
- In comparison, how much importance is placed upon innovation, individual expression, diversity, differentiation, entrepreneurship and aspiring to be distinctive, memorable and relevant?
- Do people dare to question and dissent from prevailing opinions? Do formal reviews and development activities explicitly embrace the personal qualities and skills needed to be different, craft novel offerings, and create genuine choices?
- Are people equipped with the tools needed to challenge prevailing activities and assumptions?
- Are innovations, departures from the norm and breakthroughs that create distinctive value rewarded?

- Do incentives encourage people to become more effective at playing current games, or do they inspire them to create new and alternative games?
- Are new people explicitly recruited to 'enrich the gene pool' and increase diversity?
- To what extent are the company's people, processes, knowledge, working environments and supporting infrastructure conducive of reflection and learning, distinctive and a source of differentiation from competitors?

There are many ways of creating genuine alternatives. For example, we could strike a different balance between delivery time and distinctiveness. Many of us would not make the trade-offs that certain suppliers decide on our behalf. Enthusiasts for custom-built cars forgo fuel economy from lower wind resistance and opt for designs that turn heads. Some consumers might prefer a more accessible product that has fewer features but which is easier to use and understand. Could they be offered a utility version?

Corporate communications should highlight what is special about an enterprise and its activities. Do your company's people have special competencies? Do they work and learn in novel ways? Does it have exclusive access to – or ownership of – particular know-how or unusual approaches? Do its products and services provide memorable features?

Finally, does your company help prospects to understand its unique capabilities and buy its offerings? Does it use accessible tools to assess requirements, configure and price solutions, and generate proposals? Do its people design personalized products and services? Can customers create their own offerings and 'try them out' in virtual worlds?

Differentiation requires a willingness to explore and discover. Winners are much more likely to be pioneers who dare to question. They reject bland consensus, middle ways and lowest common denominators. They think outside of the box.

Further Information

*'Shaping Things to Come, strategies for creating alternative enterprises' (2001) by Colin Coulson-Thomas, and published by Blackhall Publishing.

CHAPTER 7

WINNING
COMPETITIVE BIDS

A total of 304 companies with a combined annual turnover of over £65 billion participated in the core winning new business survey. Sectors in which competitive bidding is widespread such as construction, IT and telecommunications, engineering and transport and distribution are well represented. Panels of experts have examined bidding in particular business sectors. In addition, 62 companies participated in a separate study of 20 specific bidding for business skills. Winning competitive bids has also been examined in parallel studies of how over 500 professional firms set about obtaining new business. Specific reviews have been undertaken of the winning business processes and practices of over 100 companies.

Most businesses would like to secure a higher proportion of the contracts they bid for. Bidding is a tough game. Competitive markets and falling barriers to entry strengthen the negotiating position of buyers. As more contracts are put out to competitive tender and new entrants are invited to bid, the prospects of winning a particular opportunity can fall.

As expectations rise, invitations to tender are also becoming more demanding. Proposals get larger and more expensive to prepare. The cost of lost bids have to be recovered out of a squeezed margin on those won. Companies that win too few bids are driven out of business. Enterprises need to succeed in competitive bid situations.

Yet some companies – according to a flow of reports from the Winning Business Research and Benchmarking Programme (see Appendix A) – are much more successful than others at winning business. Studies undertaken cover sectors such as construction, engineering, manufacturing, IT and telecoms, and professions ranging from lawyers and accountants to engineering and management consultants.

The findings – which we examine in this chapter – are consistent and compelling. The approaches of the 'superstars' or winners enable them to regularly outperform the 'also rans' or losers included in bid races to 'make up the numbers'. Understanding the critical success factors for winning competitive bids and how high performers operate, and building them into winning business processes and job support tools (see also chapter 24) greatly increases the prospect of increasing overall win rates.

A wide gulf exists between winners and losers. They appear distinct species with very different attitudes and approaches. 'Losers' are undisciplined, unimaginative and reactive. They pursue far too many opportunities, and focus primarily upon their employers' concerns and priorities.

Members of 'loser' bid teams respond mechanically to invitations to tender. They are pre-occupied with the practicalities of producing proposals, such as obtaining cost information and CVs. They find themselves under pressure to meet submission deadlines. Yet they ignore tools that could speed up their basic activities and free up thinking time.

'Losers' 'hold back' and only commit significant effort when a prospect is 'seriously interested'. They describe their jobs in terms of 'submitting bids'. As winning business professionals, they actually spend their days losing potential business as most proposals sent in are rejected. In businesses with below average success rates, bid team members are left to 'get on with it'. Senior managers are rarely involved in individual opportunities.

'Losers' measure success by the number of proposals submitted. They make little effort to learn from experience or best practice. Rejection letters enable them to 'close the file' and move onto the next proposal. Above all, they don't mind losing. Failure is accepted as the norm, and rationalised with phrases such as 'you can't win them all'.

'Winners' are very different from losers. They are far more confident and proactive. They identify prospects with growth potential that would make good business partners. They take the initiative and approach those they would most like to do business with.

'Winners' ruthlessly prioritise available opportunities. Turning down some invitations to bid allows more effort to be devoted to those retained. Construction company Henry Boot suffered a fall in turnover as a result of being more selective, but profitability significantly improved.

'Winners' want their customers and prospects to do well. They become absorbed in their problems and opportunities and focus responses and structure proposals upon prospect needs, priorities and selection criteria.

When winners do respond, it is with commitment and clear objectives. They think through the outcomes and relationship they would like to achieve. They hit the ground running, and allocate sufficient resources early on to build up an unassailable lead.

Senior managers in the more successful companies participate in pitches. The visible and active support of senior management can be decisive in close contests. Redwood Publishing wrote its Managing Director into a proposal submitted to BT and won the business.

'Winners' try to understand how buying decisions are made. They identify and address the selection criteria being used. They consider the personalities involved and remain sensitive to changing buyer concerns throughout the purchasing process. They work hard to establish empathy, build trust, and match the culture of prospects. Wang successfully demonstrated 'cultural fit' prior to becoming a supplier of support services to Dell.

Where possible, 'winners' automate the more mechanical aspects of proposal production. Eyretel commissioned a laptop-based tool (see www.cotoco.com) to enable its sales reps to access presentational information, configure and price solutions, and generate proposals. Time freed up is used to tailor responses, differentiate offerings and build relationships.

At the end of the day, 'winners' want to win. They are gutted when they lose. Win or lose, they regularly review their processes and practices, and debriefs are held to learn from both successes and failures.

The results of the Winning Business Research and Benchmarking Programme suggest the winners could do even better. The 'super bidders' – the 4% who win more than three out of four of the competitive races they enter – are only very effective at less than half of the 18 critical success factors identified by the report 'Winning New Business, the critical success factors'*. Quite simply, there is enormous opportunity for most businesses to significantly improve their 'hit rate'.

The gap between 'winners' and 'losers' can be bridged. 'Win rates' are directly related to how many of the 18 key factors a company is good at.

So what should you do to increase your win rate? The 'Winning New Business, the critical success factors' report and/or the 'winning business' report for your industry or profession* spell out the relevant critical success factors. The individual reports also contain best practice case studies and commentaries by industry experts.

A related bespoke benchmarking service is also available, which allows you to compare your company's performance with both average and high achievers. The bespoke report that is generated highlights where your business is most behind the most successful bidders.

Review the skills of members of your company's bid teams. Another report produced by the Winning Business Research and Benchmarking Programme, 'Bidding for Business, the skills agenda' has identified the top twenty skills required for successful bidding and how to acquire them*. Thirty bidding tools are also available in the form of 'The Contract Bid Manager's Toolkit'*.

Consider how sales support tools could help put your message across. The problem of recruiting and training sales staff in the rapidly changing telecommunications sector was constraining Eyretel's growth. The sales support tool developed by Co*t*oco reduced the sales cycle by up to 50% and the original investment was returned within four months by just one order. This and other applications are examined in a 'Win More Business' CD-Rom that has been produced by the Winning Business Research and Benchmarking Programme team*.

Finally, regularly subject your processes and practices to an independent review. Even though there is enormous potential for improvement, many companies re-engineer almost every process except that for winning business. For example, another report 'Pricing for Profit'* from the Winning Business Research and Benchmarking Programme team shows how some companies achieve higher prices than others for similar offerings (see the next chapter). You can avoid being a 'loser' by consciously setting out to become a 'winner'.

Further information

*Information on the Winning Business Research and Benchmarking Programme and details of 'Winning New Business, the critical success factors', 'Bidding for Business, the Skills Agenda', 'The Contract Bid Manager's Toolkit', 'Pricing for Profit', the 'Winning New Business' CD-ROM and the 'Winning Business' series of reports can be obtained from Policy Publications. Tel: + 44 (0) 1733 361149; Email: colinct@tiscali.co.uk or from www.ntwkfirm.com/bookshop

CHAPTER 8

PRICE FOR PROFIT

Some of the companies that had participated in other surveys within the winning companies, winning people research programme were reluctant to discuss their pricing strategies, policies and tactics. Nevertheless 73 companies were covered by the pricing for profit survey carried out in association with the Chartered Institute of Marketing. The respondents covered a broad mix of pricing experience and included those selling in both business-to-business and business-to-consumer markets. The turnover of participating companies ranged from under £10 million (26%) to over £1 billion (8%). Another survey covering the chief executives of over 60 organisations corroborated the main findings of the pricing for profit study.

Why is it that some companies are able to charge more than their competitors for what at first sight might appear essentially the same or a very similar product? In this chapter we will examine how to command premium prices for your offerings.

Pricing decisions impact directly upon sales revenues and profitability. Charge too much and orders are lost, while charging too little erodes margins and may give the impression that offerings are of low quality.

Obtaining and sustaining higher prices ought to be a top priority of entrepreneurs. Yet often they agonize over perfecting what is sold and then take quick pricing decisions based largely on guesswork.

So how should businesses set prices? Hitherto pricing has been shrouded in mystery. Firms have either been reluctant to reveal their approaches or – particularly when less successful – they have been sensitive to the lack of rigour involved.

The author has persuaded 73 companies to reveal their pricing strategies, tactics and practices. The firms surveyed provided data on 127 factors that could affect pricing decisions. The findings set out in the report 'Pricing for Profit'* reveal that more effective pricing could boost the profitability of many companies.

Comparing the companies that are most successful at using pricing to achieve business objectives such as growing market share or improving profitability (the winners or leaders) with the least successful (the losers or laggards) reveals stark differences between the two groups. For example, leaders make more use of all nine tools and techniques examined. Over twice as many make "very extensive" use of competitor analysis. Leaders are ahead by two to one or more in their use of break-even analysis, economic value analysis and price sensitivity measurement.

The winners or leaders understand the strategic importance of pricing and are more attuned to factors such as perceived value that affect price sensitivity. Overall, sales management, marketing, sales force personnel and finance are the groups most involved in pricing. However, leaders involve a wider range of departments in pricing decisions and members of the sales team play a more significant role.

Marketing and sales should contribute to pricing as they ought to be close to customers. But left to themselves they may be tempted to 'buy' orders. Offering discounts may be regarded by losers as a softer option than differentiating, tailoring and delivering extra value to justify a higher price. However, excessive discounting can reduce profitability.

The most successful companies – our winners – rely upon evidence rather than hunch. Thus before pricing products as a line rather than individually, they would calculate whether an increase in profit overall would exceed the costs of implementation and any reductions in profit on individual products that might occur.

Leaders attempt to sell on value as opposed to price. They are more likely to segment a market-place and take a long-term view, for example using 'penetration pricing' to enter a new market. When laggards look ahead it is often for defensive reasons, for example our losers may cut prices to hold onto market share.

The cost drivers of leaders and laggards are very different. Leaders are five times more likely to increase volume to achieve economies of scale. In contrast, laggards are more likely to reduce product costs to allow price cuts or special discounts. Leaders are more realistic when allocating costs and more likely to understand the direct and indirect costs attributable to a particular product or service.

Overall leaders adopt a very different approach to building their businesses. They focus on each market segment, differentiate their offerings, and look for ways of increasing quality and delivering improved customer service. Investing in these areas allows them to build sales volume, reduce unit costs and become more competitive.

Leaders keep their pricing structures simple and transparent. Increasing an offering's economic value and the extent to which it is unique or special enables them to price for value. Differentiated, tailored and exclusive offerings attract a premium.

Laggards put the most emphasis upon cost cutting, while leaders strive to add value to their core offering, develop a reputation for service and use pricing to build closer relationships with strategic customers and key accounts. They are more willing to enter into partnering arrangements.

Pricing tactics should support business development strategy. Thus prestige pricing can enhance perceived value.

Within an economic region such as the euro zone, cross-border buying and Europe-wide purchasing are increasing the demand for pan-regional (e.g. European) prices. Companies can resist downward pressure by developing clear benefits in each market and segmenting customers into ring-fenced pan-regional groups.

Too often pricing is handled in an ad hoc and uncoordinated way. A balance may have to be struck between the centralized response demanded by major customers, and the decentralization needed to respond to local market conditions.

Automating the more routine aspects of pricing can reduce the risk of errors and free-up time for creating bespoke responses. Smart firms monitor trends and developments that may impact on prices. For example, they are alert to possible price hot spots that might trigger consumer militancy.

Overall, winners put greater effort into pricing. They use more techniques and a wider range of sources of price information. They keep their finger on the pulse of customer, user and industry opinion, and review their approaches, strategies and tactics as situations and circumstances change.

Further Information

* 'Pricing for Profit … the Critical Success Factors' by Colin Coulson-Thomas is published by Policy Publications.

CHAPTER 9

DEVELOPING STRATEGIC CUSTOMERS AND KEY ACCOUNTS

PROCESSES AND PRACTICES FOR EFFECTIVE ACCOUNT MANAGEMENT

A total of 194 companies with a combined turnover of more than £70 billion participated in the developing strategic customers and key accounts survey which was carried out in association with Marketing Business, the magazine for the Chartered Institute of Marketing. The annual turnovers of the companies ranged from under £50 million (39%) to over £1 billion (11%). 45 per cent of the participating organisations were service providers, 42 per cent were manufacturers, and 10 per cent were wholesalers or retailers. Aspects of managing relationships with customers were also examined in the course of other surveys, such as those of over 500 professional services organisations, and project work with particular companies.

Having won a valuable new customer the next challenge – which we will examine in this chapter – is to build a relationship that will result in a flow of repeat orders and follow-on business. To do this requires effective customer and/or account management, and critical success factors for building strategic customer relationships should be built into the appropriate processes and support tools.

A research team led by the author has examined how companies develop strategic customers and key accounts. The resulting report* identifies a variety of critical success factors that distinguish 'winners', the companies in the top quarter of achievement that realise the benefits of strategic customer relationships, from the 'losers' in the bottom quarter that do not. It draws upon the experiences of 194 companies with a combined turnover of over £70 billion.

The investigation by the winning business research team reveals general dissatisfaction with performance. Less than one in six of the participants consider themselves 'very effective' at increasing profitability through strategic relationships and fewer than one in seven are happy with the way they develop them. Yet, a clear majority of the respondents believe the proportion of their sales due to key accounts will increase beyond the current level of over two thirds.

The survey also reveals a wide gulf between the attitudes, approaches and results of the 'winners' and 'losers'. For example, 'winners' consider three times as many of the key processes identified by the investigating team to be 'very important', and are five times as likely to be intending to make use of emerging technologies.

'Losers' tend to live for the moment and are driven by the prospect of immediate business. They apply the 'key account' label to their most important current customers, and when dealing with them focus upon their own requirements. They use their customers to achieve their own short-term targets. Within such companies key account relationships are left to sales and marketing staff who play 'me-too' and 'catch-up with competitors'.

The 'losers' mouth generalisations about the importance of building closer relationships with customers, but do little to make them happen. They avoid commitment and integration. Open book accounting and direct electronic links are 'no go' areas. They are also very reluctant to bend standard procedures. Little effort is made to categorise accounts or 'do things differently' to help particular customers.

'Losers' use a range of traditional sales and negotiation techniques that fail to recognise 'buyer power'. Terms of business are used as a selling tool. Not surprisingly, losers are taken to the cleaners by customers who – on learning that they have become a 'key account' – respond by demanding price reductions.

The contrast between 'winners' and 'losers' is particularly stark when it comes to locking out the competition (or locking customers in). The 'winners' rank 11 out of 17 'lock out' factors examined by the research team while the 'losers' do not rank any. Quite simply the bottom quarter of companies in the survey sample do not appear to be taking any steps to protect their key accounts. No wonder they fail to realise strategic relationship benefits.

In contrast, 'winners' look ahead and take a lifetime view of relationships. They consider future potential when categorising accounts. They value their customers and are prepared to put themselves out for them. They are open and build personal relationships. Their focus is upon customer requirements and buyer expectations. They understand their customers' businesses, industries and buying processes and look out for opportunities that might benefit them.

'Losers' are sometimes exposed when particular individuals change jobs. 'Winners' encourage a broader range of contacts at multiple levels between their own staff and those of key account customers. At the same time, senior management are involved in important negotiations. They are prepared to differentiate and depart from the norm in order to deliver greater value and benefit their customers' businesses. Traditional sales techniques are largely ignored, as 'winners' influence buying rather than overtly sell.

Rather than mouth generalisations, 'winners' concentrate upon specifics. They are prepared to commit, to extend partnership to the terms of business, and to integrate processes and systems. Not surprisingly they realise the many benefits of strategic customer relationships that elude the 'losers'.

Overall, the research findings reveal that while there is a wide spectrum of effectiveness there is also considerable potential for improvement. Even the winners could do much better.

So what needs to be done? In many companies account managers have prime responsibility for customer relationship management and business development through cross selling and winning new accounts within sectors for which they are responsible. Sales directors and members of the sales team should start by defining or reviewing the role of account and/or key account managers and agreeing their responsibilities in relation to those of colleagues in order to identify and address any gaps, overlaps and boundary issues.

A profile of the competencies and 'role model' behaviours required by an effective account manager should also be developed and agreed, and individuals assessed against the agreed profile to identify personal and team development needs. Important next steps are to:

- Define and agree a key account development plan format and process, a customer relationship management process, and a process for winning business in competitive situations.
- Develop or acquire the approaches, tools and techniques account managers will require to cross sell and win and retain accounts. These include the 30 tools in the 'The Contract Bid Managers Toolkit', the 20 skills in 'Bidding for Business, the Skills Agenda' and the systematic model approach to key account management set out in the report 'Developing Strategic Customers & Key Accounts'*.
- Provide whatever training is required by the account managers, individually or as a group. Collaborative arrangements can supplement skills, experience and reference sites in areas of relative deficiency.
- Allocate existing customers and eligible prospects to individual account managers. The allocation should reflect the sectors in which the individuals and the company and its partners have particular expertise and distinctive strengths. Rules, arrangements and terms covering the availability of, access to, and use of partner know-how and staff by account managers for business development, customer support and service delivery purposes may need to be negotiated.
- Set and agree revenue and profitability targets for each sector/ account manager, and develop sector specific business development and marketing plans, account development plans for all existing key accounts, and account capture plans for all eligible target accounts.

The Winning Business Research Programme led by the author (see Appendix A) has produced reports on the critical success factors for winning business in particular business sectors and various professions, and account managers can use these to identify 'best practice' approaches. Specific sector and cross sector applications, offerings, events and marketing materials may also need to be developed.

Sales and business development teams should establish mechanisms for capturing, sharing and learning from positive and negative experiences. Joining a network such as the Business Development Forum may allow account managers to learn from the experiences of their peers. Deficiencies should be addressed. Thus arrangements could be negotiated with non-national partners to support the winning of international accounts.

Each account manager should be responsible for prioritising new business opportunities and prospects, allocating and managing available business development resources, and achieving account and sector business development and profitability targets. The assignment of customers to account managers will ensure a single point of contact, and help to create a holistic insight into the totality of customers' business needs.

Finally, sales directors must ensure that an appropriate performance management framework is in place. In addition to regular measures of customer satisfaction, retention and loyalty, performance indicators should address certain lessons of the research investigation*. For example:

- How much time do account managers spend in the office as opposed to with customers and prospects?
- Do senior staff and colleagues in other areas actively support relationship building with key accounts?
- What forms of interdependence with customers and integration of systems and processes have been achieved?
- Are account managers and other staff learning from and with strategic customers?
- Are risks and opportunities being shared?
- Are partnering relationships being built and open book accounting practised?

The latter questions are important. The growth of partnering, spread of e-commerce, and desire for strategic alliances were identified by respondents to the 'Developing Strategic Customers & Key Accounts' survey as the three most important issues they face. Cautious companies that avoid risks by staying with what they know and adopt legalistic and protective approaches are likely to end up as low margin commodity suppliers. Playing 'win–lose' games ensures they lose.

Those who are flexible, innovative, willing to accept challenges, and ready to adopt new ways of working and learning earn higher returns. 'Winners' are willing to adopt a partnership approach. They share visions and risks. They strive for 'win–win' outcomes by agreeing mutually beneficial objectives. They remain relevant and add value.

'Winners' are prepared to commit to continued and measured improvements in whatever they supply or provide. Savings achieved are shared between the parties concerned. If required, they practise 'open book' accounting. They also recognise that differences can and do arise. However, within the partnering relationships they foster there are simple and quick processes for handling disputes at the lowest possible levels. Their earn respect and engender loyalty. Their relationships last and prosper.

Further Information

*'Developing Strategic Customers & Key Accounts', 'The Contract Bid Managers Toolkit', 'Bidding for Business, the Skills Agenda', the 'Close to the Customer' series of briefings, related reports in the 'Winning Business' series and bespoke key account benchmarking reports can be obtained from Policy Publications. Tel: +44 (0) 1733 361149; Email: colinct@tiscali.co.uk or from www.ntwkfirm.com/bookshop

CHAPTER 10

NEGOTIATING PARTNERING RELATIONSHIPS

FROM CONFRONTATION TO COLLABORATION

The desire for improved collaboration and partnering has emerged in studies of both purchasing and building relationships with customers within the winning companies, winning people research programme. 490 organisations participated in these two investigations. Other studies within the programme – and projects with particular companies – have examined processes, technologies and tools that can support more effective collaboration.

Some companies focus so much upon competing that they overlook the importance of collaboration. In the last chapter we considered how to build closer relationships with important customers. In this chapter we will also examine the importance of working with other organizations. For example, business, channel and supply chain partners could collaborate in the production of sales support tools.

Shared costs and increases in productivity and performance across a wider range of joint activity can significantly enhance financial returns. The chances of cooperation may be boosted by conscious effort to create a partnering relationship, in which mutually beneficial outcomes are negotiated and benefits are shared.

Winning business teams setting out to build relationships with customers and potential business partners sometimes assume a degree of harmony between organizations that may not exist. The various parties to new business and partnering negotiations may not be of one mind. The negotiation challenge may be to move from confrontation to collaboration by helping those involved to articulate their interests, understand contrary positions and conclude mutually acceptable accommodation.

Detailed and final negotiations can open up a Pandora's Box of arguments and lead to disagreements, disputes and confrontation between contending viewpoints. Latent conflicts may be brought to the surface. Supply chain partners may display protective behaviour. Different interests may seek to use meetings for their own ends. New ways may need to be found to handle disagreements and reconcile differing requirements.

Sensitive negotiators recognize that people may have different perceptions of the desirability, direction and consequences of certain outcomes. Some may feel strongly about certain issues. Old debates, clashes of personality, divisions within the boardroom or tensions between sales channel partners may be brought to the surface.

Within many markets there is a legacy of distrust and much scope for misunderstanding between negotiating parties and head offices and operating units. Some may harbour suspicions that particular groups are seeking to benefit from changes at the expense of others. Certain partners may feel they are being asked to absorb an unfair proportion of budget cuts or make a disproportionate contribution.

Winning business and partnering negotiators should endeavour to identify differing expectations and perspectives and anticipate potential flash points. There might be varying degrees of misunderstanding between national cultures and distinct minorities within an international organization or marketplace. The greater the diversity between the different parties to a negotiation the more likely it is that outcomes may need to reflect local situations.

Possible arenas of confrontation need to be recognized and likely conflicts addressed. New business and corporate communications can themselves become a source of distrust and tension, especially when words are not consistent with deeds. People may perceive a gap between rhetoric and reality. For example, corporate messages might stress the need to adopt a longer-term approach to the building of partnering relationships with customers while directors take short-term actions to cut costs.

The author's research programme (see Introduction, page xv) has examined the approaches of a wide range of organizations in many sectors and identified critical success factors for managing change, competing and winning*. The findings reveal that successful companies or 'winners' display attitudes and behaviours for building relationships and partnerships that differ from those of 'losers' or businesses that struggle.

Successful and unsuccessful companies pursue very different approaches to avoiding disputes, handling confrontation and encouraging collaboration. People associated with 'loser' companies are cautious collaborators. They stress the time, effort and expense required to establish and build relationships, and they often conclude that the likely results do not justify the investment required.

In making such choices, losers act as though working with others is an option rather than a necessity. At heart they are reluctant to share and would prefer to operate alone. They keep to themselves in an attempt to avoid becoming entangled in rivalries and drawn into disputes.

When negotiating, losers pursue divisive strategies and seek to benefit at the expense of other parties. They sometimes foment conflicts in order to achieve sectional interests.

Some losers prize their independence so much they pass-up opportunities to grow that would require them to work with colleagues and business partners. Collaboration is seen as a constraint upon their freedom of action.

Losers settle into familiar ways of operating. If existing arrangements and practices appear to work reasonably well they are reluctant to consider alternatives that might offer additional benefits.

Winners are more willing to work with colleagues and are more likely to be prepared to co-operate with other complementary suppliers. They see and seek the advantages of collaboration. It might enable them to learn and develop. It may allow them to offer a wider range of services to their customers and pursue a broader range of opportunities.

Winners are usually receptive to approaches from others. They are open to new ideas. They welcome suggestions for improvements and innovation. They actively search for potential business partners and explore possibilities for joint initiatives or collective action.

Once contact is established winners do not mind the confrontation and argument that may be needed to create mutual respect and a meeting of minds. They endeavour to find common ground, resolve conflicts and promote shared interests and goals.

Collaboration extends to 'external' parties. As companies outsource and focus upon core competencies they may hive off or transfer various activities to specialist suppliers. As a consequence combinations of complementary organisations work together in supply chains rather than operate alone as single entities to deliver value to customers. Each concentrates upon what it does best. A company that endeavours to do everything itself may become a 'jack of all trades and master of none'.

Consortium responses to invitations to tender for complex and large-scale projects are also increasingly common in certain sectors. Only by working together may the respondents be able to assemble the capabilities required. Companies that collaborate with business partners may significantly improve their prospects of winning a major contract.

It helps if aspiring collaborators have compatible interests and complementary capabilities. When they need to work with others, losers tend to seek out potential collaborators with similar characteristics to themselves. As a consequence, they sometimes find in crisis situations that the whole is not necessarily greater than the sum of the parts. Like drunks endeavouring to prop each other up, they compound each other's weaknesses.

If the parties endeavouring to co-operate are very different they may not have enough in common to cement a relationship. On the other hand, if they are so alike as to add little to each other's capabilities collaboration may not be justified. Winners are more likely to understand that lasting relationships often involve dissimilar but complementary partners that allocate roles and responsibilities according to comparative advantage.

Losers tend to be essentially selfish where relationships are concerned. They seek to co-operate on their terms, and they often put the bare minimum of effort into maintaining them.

Within relationships losers hold back emotionally and intellectually and endeavour not to become too deeply involved. They are wary and may even undertake cost-benefit assessments. When negotiating they endeavour to 'score points' and adopt win–lose approaches.

Collaborative 'partnerships' can take various forms. Whether an informal arrangement or a formal joint venture, such relationships can be of great importance. Opportunities can be addressed and significant amounts of new business won as a result of co-operative action. The consortium bid for a major contract, with each member focusing upon an area of core expertise, is increasingly acceptable and may be encouraged.

Winners work hard at reaping the benefits of co-operation. They commit the effort required to establish and regularly review collaborative processes and practices. For example, they may put practical arrangements in place to clarify the ownership of customers, prevent poaching and protect intellectual property.

Winners also recognise that if internal and external relationships are to grow and deepen they should be acceptable and mutually beneficial to all the parties involved. Instinctively, when negotiating they look for win–win outcomes.

Winners also avoid rushing. Some parties will take longer to adjust and integrate than others. Winners also understand the dynamic nature of associations and arrangements. Time, effort and care may need to be devoted to them if they are to become more intimate.

Winners willingly commit. They become involved. They are flexible and understanding, and prepared to do things differently to accommodate particular and legitimate interests. They are also not 'fair weather friends'. They can be relied upon in crisis situations.

Collaboration should not be pursued at any cost or become a distraction. Some losers devote great effort to achieving 'teamwork' that may conceal or sideline differences and gloss over concerns in order to achieve a bland consensus.

Winners adopt a more entrepreneurial approach. They encourage open and frank discussion. They become demanding collaborators and partners. On occasion they may create waves in order to make faster progress.

Overall winners recognise that a lack of tension may mean the absence of ambition. The quiet organization may be asleep. Their drive and desire to innovate and push back the boundaries of what is possible may provoke confrontation between those favouring the status quo and those who desire to move on. The need for activities and processes for building mutual understanding, reconciling differences and building collaborative relationships is understood and addressed.

Discussion, informed debate, a willingness to challenge and a degree of confrontation is sometimes desirable. It can prevent complacency, spur innovation and lead to higher performance. Disputes are usually better in the open – where efforts can be made to resolve them – than hidden when they can fester.

It may be possible to avoid some conflicts by ring fencing certain activities or giving one or more of the protagonists greater autonomy. Involving different parties in discussions at proposal or concept stage may give them an opportunity to flag up areas of possible difficulty. Although their participation might delay a decision, implementation may be speeded up due to the greater perceived legitimacy of the process and likely outcomes made more acceptable.

Possible mechanisms can range from an ad hoc discussion forum or inter-unit team to a partnering agreement or issue monitoring and management. A process may also be required for handling dysfunctional conflicts. This could provide a framework for identifying common ground, isolating points of difference, and assessing and addressing the root causes of disputes. Organizational boundaries may need to be redrawn, roles and responsibilities reallocated, processes re-engineered and strategies reviewed.

Winning new business and customer relations teams can play a key role in moving from a climate of confrontation to a culture of collaboration. They can identify supporters and opponents of change and endeavour to ensure each understands the other's viewpoints and legitimate concerns. They can put feedback loops in place and encourage senior managers to listen. They can assess tolerance for diversity and whether sufficient discussion and debate is occurring.

Business development teams and key account managers should work to achieve mutual respect and the credibility of two-way communications. Colleagues should be encouraged to match words with deeds. They need to distinguish between disruptive opposition and constructive questioning and encourage the latter.

Finally, customers and business partners should also be encouraged and helped to raise concerns, express viewpoints, explore issues, reconcile opinions, foster collaboration and share learning. Open relationships based upon trust and mutual respect are conducive of mutually beneficial co-operation.

Further Information

* 'Transforming the Company, Manage Change, Compete and Win' (2002) by Colin Coulson-Thomas is available from Kogan Page.

CHAPTER 11

MANAGING SUPPLY CHAIN RELATIONSHIPS

The effective management of supply chain relationships emerged as a key factor in surveys undertaken within the wining companies, winning people research programme of both quality and performance improvement. Over 300 organisations participated in these studies. A survey of how 194 companies build strategic and key customer relationships revealed how supply chain relationships can be used to lock customers in and competitors out. However, the investigation of corporate learning within the programme found that few of the education, training and learning activities managed by the 69 people interviewed embraced business partners within their organisation's supply chains

How effective are you at working with other businesses? Following on from research findings we considered in the last chapter, should you be learning to collaborate as well as compete? Early industrial tycoons used to grow their firms by 'integrating along the supply chain' or grabbing more of what other companies did. Some verged on megalomania and aspired to take over just about anything that moved.

Today's commercial world is very different. Customers and investors look for 'focus'. They expect businesses to concentrate upon what they do best. Non-core activities are outsourced. Firms that spread themselves too thinly risk becoming 'Jack of all trades and master of none'.

Customers are also more demanding. They want the best. The emphasis has switched to differentiation and specialisation, doing a smaller number of things supremely well and developing a reputation for excellence in a particular field.

In business, sport and the arts an ever-higher share of the available rewards accrue to those who are outstanding. Average performers are marginalized while the super-stars clean up. As markets become more complex and competitive there are just not enough hours in the day to keep up with everything.

Inevitably these developments mean we have to change how we operate. We can no longer afford to keep to ourselves or go it alone. A greater proportion of the value consumed by end customers is now delivered by collective endeavours.

Co-operation with other firms enables businesses to broaden offerings with complementary products, add services to justify premium prices or reach new customers. Like it or not, companies have to work ever more closely with business partners. In many markets good supply chain relationships – the subject of this chapter – are a critical success factor.

The reputations of brands reflect customers' total experience. A failing at one point can undermine excellence elsewhere. Hence, the importance of working together to ensure consistency of service and create a positive spiral of mutual re-enforcement.

Managing supply chain relationships should be high on the entrepreneur's agenda. An investigation led by the author* reveals that visionaries use them to create new business opportunities while competitors wedded to existing practices go under. Successful companies (winners) reshape their organisations, introduce new channels and establish new markets through more intimate relationships with customers, suppliers and business partners.

Despite the opportunities, many businesses lack ambition. They tinker with existing processes and adopt-me-too practices rather than innovate. The creativity displayed when crafting new offerings is not matched by similar imagination when they consider how to get these into the hands of customers.

Of course change for its own sake should be avoided. As we will see in the next chapter, it can be disruptive of existing relationships while new ones take time and effort to establish. Significant change should be for a strategic purpose, and one that can be shared by supply chain partners. The focus should be upon the customer, for example offering them additional choice or more tailored products and services.

Providing alternatives to existing provision can help to differentiate a business from its competitors. If more customers demand distinct or bespoke offerings, supply chain partners must deliver greater variety at lower costs and more quickly. Ways of reducing waiting time might range from joint R&D and taskforces to seamless processes and direct electronic links.

On-line ordering, just-in-time responses, the ability to track orders and 'help-desk' support can all help to lock customers in. Maybe invoices and reports could be delivered electronically in formats to suit individual customers. Contracted-in experts might be able to provide additional specialist services.

Collaboration can speed up international expansion. For example, it is difficult to become a global software player without a strong market position in North America. A local presence may be required. This might involve giving further percentages to yet more partners, but the smaller proportion retained may be of much larger income streams.

Micro-businesses – even individual craft workers in the jungle – can reach a global clientele via the Internet. Working with website management, transaction processing, fulfilment and debt collection partners frees them from the distractions of hiring people, finding premises and putting support processes in place. Instead, they concentrate upon their individual passions and play to their particular strengths.

Winners innovate. They create new ways of doing businesses and additional routes to potential customers. Maybe airline passengers and travellers on intercity trains could order goods from an electronic catalogue and pick them up on arrival at their destinations. People could collect items selected on an office PC from reception when they leave to go home.

A particular role within a supply chain may both create a new source of competitive advantage and represent a wider business opportunity. For example, a service such as handling warranty repairs could be opened up to suppliers of non-competing products. A further partner could be brought in to run an interest group or offer end customers discounts on related items.

So long as rewards exceed costs and image and reputation are enhanced rather than compromised, additional service providers can improve the competitive positioning of a supply chain. Yet few such groupings manage their affairs as a whole and actively seek new members, even though competition is increasingly between networks of collaborating partners rather than individual companies.

Some companies develop multiple supply chains as they further segment their customers and diversify their channels to market. Each additional relationship can complicate the task of securing agreement. Supply chains can fragment as well as coalesce. Participants need to be alert to potential fissures and forces for fragmentation.

Particular partners may seek to cut out intermediaries and secure a more direct route to an end-customer, perhaps via e-business over the Internet. Others may review their core competencies and consolidate their relationships. A whole network might be made redundant by the replacement of a physical market place by an electronic market space.

Supply chains do not obviate the search for advantage and profit. Today's collaborator may become tomorrow's competitor. Relationships should be regularly reviewed. Are they meeting end customer needs? Do they enable participants to specialise and build up their core skills?

Inevitably differences will arise. The trick is not to avoid or ignore them. Frustration, misunderstanding and resentment may build to a level that alienates one or more business partners. The whole chain is only as effective as its weakest link. A low-level dispute resolution process should be put in place to tackle issues before they escalate and entrenched positions are taken.

Losers sometimes naively exaggerate their own worth to others. Companies should be realistic about the value of their own contribution within a supply chain. Is it visible to end customers? How might their changing requirements, emerging trends and new technologies affect it? New attitudes, skills and capabilities may be required to deal with future challenges.

Particular attention should be paid to the likely impact of economic cycles and technological developments with the potential to change the shape of markets and create new ones. Businesses need to think about the implications for their relationships with supply chain partners and any new ground rules that are likely to apply.

Smart entrepreneurs build partnering relationships with both customers and suppliers. Winners start with requirements, what end-customers would really like. They identify gaps in their own capabilities and their partners' collective capacity to deliver. While acknowledging their deficiencies they do not lose sleep over them. Instead they co-operate with complementary providers of whatever they lack.

Cooperation with others may involve letting go of certain activities and possibilities. This can be difficult for entrepreneurs who feel they are losing part of 'their' opportunity. Many losers instinctively dislike sharing.

In reality, many business founders soon face pressure from investors to be 'true to themselves'. They are asked to focus upon their unique qualities and personal strengths and bring in people with complementary skills, or even hand over the reigns to professional managers. In essence, putting new supply chain relationships in place is specialisation at the enterprise level.

When they negotiate, effective collaborators flush out the key business objectives of the various parties involved and agree 'win–win' outcomes that are mutually beneficial to all concerned. Winners recognise that relationships which are too one-sided do not stand the test of time.

If cost savings and productivity gains are shared, business partners have more of an incentive to work together. It is usually to everyone's advantage to act in the best interests of a supply chain as a whole. It may be helpful for the parties to formally contract to achieve certain targeted improvements over time.

Resilient relationships are based upon openness and trust. This may extend to open book accounting to dispel suspicions of 'excess profits'. Everybody usually benefits if all business partners do well. The attention of parties that secure inadequate returns may wander. Collective success can generate the funds to invest in technology upgrades and other means of securing continuing competitive advantage.

Further Information

*'The Competitive Network' report and methodology shows how to combine e-business with re-engineering to build value creating supply chains and win new markets. Details and information on the related 'The Responsive Organisation' re-engineering methodology 'for introducing new ways of working' can be obtained from Policy Publications.

CHAPTER 12

LEADING AND MANAGING CHANGE

A total of 163 companies employing over four and a quarter million people participated in the initial surveys of changing organisations. Of the organisations examined, 79 had a turnover of over £1 billion, and over 60% of survey respondents were chairmen, chief executives or managing directors. Subsequent investigations have examined particular aspects of managing change, for example the role of communications, teamwork, project management or particular management techniques such as quality or re-engineering. Over 500 companies have participated in these surveys, while parallel studies of directors and boards have also examined their role in leading change and transformation.

When considering performance improvement, business development, re-engineering and transformation options, boards need to achieve a balance between change and continuity, and focus upon areas of greatest opportunity. As situations alter and circumstances change, capabilities, processes and working practices need to be reviewed. For many, change is an inevitable consequence of their roles and responsibilities. It may be both necessary and desirable, and the management of it is now a lucrative area for consultants.

However certain changes are more welcome than others, and some people are much better at managing them than their peers. In some companies managers may be assessed and rewarded according to the amount of change they bring about. However, directors, boards and senior managers should tread warily as change can be disruptive and costly. It can distract people who should be focused upon other priorities.

When mismanaged, change can be stressful and destructive. Few changes affect everyone in the same way, and the impacts of certain changes may not be immediately apparent. There might be hidden and longer term consequences. Board members may be divided between those who are for or against particular changes. People who are indifferent or ambivalent may simply 'go with the flow'.

Despite much rhetoric about 'change management' and nimble, responsive and flexible organizations, many business leaders periodically downsize, regularly restructure and inexorably destroy shareholder wealth. The research programme led by the author (see Introduction, page xv) has sought to find out why there is such a wide gulf between intentions and outcomes. The findings set out in 'Transforming the Company'* identify what needs to be done.

Frustration is the inevitable consequence of how many people set about managing change. Many unsuccessful companies or losers introduce far too many changes. People are unsettled and important relationships are disrupted. Problems are allowed to fester until a point at which dramatic restructurings may be forced by the pressure of events.

Smart boards make adaptation and change a way of life. Winners read the road ahead and try to anticipate changes that may be required. They identify and approach those whose help they might need. They are proactive rather than reactive, and retain control. They introduce required changes when there is the greatest chance of success.

Much will depend upon the purposes of change and the capacity of the people involved to adapt. Directors should question the rationale for proposed changes, and ask whether an impact analysis has been undertaken of their likely implications. Are the potential consequences for employees, customers, suppliers, business partners and investors adequately assessed?

When deciding what to change, don't confuse operational and strategic issues, or your personal interests with those of the organisation. Build an effective board of competent directors who understand the distinction between direction and management. Surround yourself with open-minded, pragmatic and competent contributors who will consider proposals for change dispassionately and objectively.

Particular attention should be paid to the interests of customers. When new models are introduced will the spare parts needed for earlier products still be available? Introducing changes without considering their costs or consequences can do great harm to reputations and relationships. Customers sometimes have more regard for a company's offerings than its managers.

An 'end-to-end' perspective is required. People need to think through the likely consequences of changes for colleagues and business partners. Altering a task at one point in a process, or introducing a new activity, may cause problems for those operating elsewhere, either within the same process or in a related or dependent one.

Allies and opponents need to be identified. Some champion change. Others undermine it. Change can disorientate and disrupt, even when it is beneficial. People may also only be able to take so much of it. Organisational leaders need to think carefully about how much change they can handle before negative consequences wipe out desired gains.

Change for change's sake should be avoided. A degree of continuity may be required. People in smart organisations led by winners build upon an existing reputation and safeguard core values. Steps may need to be taken to protect what is important and prevent the compromise of cherished beliefs. What are the anchor points of the business? What is the cement that holds its people together?

There are other questions to consider. Might changes result in the loss of strategically important knowledge and understanding? Is sufficient effort devoted to building longer-term relationships with customers, suppliers, investors and business partners? How easy is it for people to speak up against change?

Directors should distinguish between goals, values, objectives, policies and activities that need to be changed and those that should be continued. Too many people passively 'follow the herd'. Once a clear majority appears to favour a particular course of action, they climb aboard the prevailing bandwagon.

Think also about longer term and strategic impacts. Imitating and copying others can be dangerous. People can sometimes be naïve or mistaken regarding their best long-term interests. Preferences and priorities can change. Nothing is more frustrating than finding certain options have been lost because a decision cannot be reversed.

Boards sometimes attempt to change too much. Is there sufficient continuity for people to have a sense of identity, belonging, direction and purpose? Are conscious efforts made to provide enough continuity for people not to feel threatened and insecure?

Certain rules of thumb emerge from the 'Transforming the Company' study. Present a compelling case for change. People should only be expected to make demanding changes for good reason. The visions and rationales offered by many boards are excessively general. Inspire and motivate with a distinctive vision, compelling purpose and clear objectives. Accentuate the positive. Sell the benefits, but avoid blather and hype.

Think through 'what's in it' for those involved. People should be encouraged and enabled to work and learn in whatever ways best enable them to harness their full potential and give of their best. Individuals differ in how they react to certain situations and opportunities. Thus working from home may not be suitable for those who are not inwardly directed or self-motivated.

Effort should be concentrated where it is most likely to make a difference. Justifiable changes are more likely to be those that focus upon the critical success factors for achieving key corporate objectives and delivering greater customer and shareholder value. Winning business is particularly important for ambitious companies.

People need to be motivated, prepared, and equipped to achieve the changes they are expected to bring about. However, while general 'change' programmes are becoming more common, bespoke initiatives and specific tools to help individuals bring about particular changes are few and far between. More effort needs to be devoted to them.

Think carefully too about how much change your team can handle. Change can disorientate even when it is beneficial. After a point, negative consequences may wipe out desired gains. At the same time, don't underestimate the potential of your colleagues. Be prepared to trust them and, when it is reasonable to do so, take calculated risks.

Changes occurring all around us represent challenges and opportunities. Boards should consider who are likely to be 'gainers' and 'losers' from significant trends and developments and assess whether new or alternative offerings would mitigate undesirable impacts or enable people to take fuller advantage of emerging possibilities. Those affected might represent a lucrative potential market for products and services tailored to their particular interests.

As a business grows its directors may be unable to become directly involved in the many and varied activities that more bespoke and imaginative responses to a greater variety of requirements demand. Organisations need to transform themselves into incubators of creative solutions and communities of entrepreneurs. Teams should be enabled to bring about whatever changes are required to enable them to achieve their objectives and deliver value to *their* customers.

Those who endeavour to bring about ambitious and fundamental changes should expect to encounter setbacks. Persist. Be confident, determined, pragmatic and positive. Value constructive criticism and invite feedback. Don't rationalize disappointment. Learn from it. Achieving transformational change is often easier and usually more satisfying than rationalizing, managing and suffering the consequences of failure.

Further Information

*'Transforming the Company, Manage Change, Compete and Win' (2002) by Colin Coulson-Thomas is available from Kogan Page.

CHAPTER 13

CORPORATE TRANSFORMATION

The research undertaken in the area of corporate transformation has drawn upon the studies mentioned in chapter 12 concerning different aspects of leading and managing change, including specific studies of directors and boards. Additional work included involvement in over 100 change and transformation programmes, and a pan-European investigation of differing approaches to bringing about fundamental change. This encompassed an examination of over 40 re-engineering and transformation methodologies. Subsequent workshops have assessed and compared different approaches with a view to determining those which are most appropriate in particular situations and contexts.

Some companies succeed. They adapt to changing circumstances, and they remain relevant and vital. Their people manage change, compete and win.

Other companies struggle and stagnate. They adopt fashionable approaches. They buy the latest technologies. They introduce generic or re-engineered processes, and they are advised by leading professional firms. Yet they still fail.

In the last chapter we looked at the leadership of change. In this chapter we consider how to handle situations in which more radical action is needed, i.e. more than evolutionary adjustment or continuous improvement is required

Have you ever wondered why some companies are less successful than others in similar circumstances at introducing transformational change? What are these people overlooking or doing wrong? What do the winners do differently? To answer these questions the research programme led by the author (see Introduction, page xv) has been examining the corporate transformation experience of companies for more than a decade.

As mentioned in chapter 1, research teams have examined key processes such as those for winning business, building relationships and creating and exploiting knowledge. The outcomes achieved by survey participants are ranked from the most to the least successful, and the approaches of the 'winners' or most successful are compared with the 'losers' or least successful to isolate the factors that make a difference. The results summarized in: 'Transforming the Company, Manage Change, Compete and Win'* suggest most of the critical success factors are attitudinal and behavioural.

Encouragingly, there is enormous scope for improvement. Typically, even the most successful companies are only very effective at less than a half of the critical success factors examined. This suggests there is enormous scope for improving the performance of key processes. By adopting winning behaviours, many companies could achieve step change increases in performance in important areas of corporate operation.

Let's look at some overall differences between the behaviours of those in key positions who fail and succeed respectively at bringing about a fundamental transformation of their organizations.

First, we will examine the losers. They are indecisive and oblivious to the needs of others. They are cautious, wary of commitments and fail to inspire and motivate. They are also reactive. They respond to events and often fail to anticipate the need to change.

Losers are indifferently led. Boards confuse operational and strategic issues. They offer bland rhetoric and spin rather than a compelling vision and clear direction. When they do act it is often in peripheral areas. They overlook what is important and the biggest opportunities for performance improvement.

Losers hoard information. They are reluctant to delegate and trust. Although driven by their own agendas they often end up playing other people's games. They adopt standard approaches and are rigid and inflexible. They imitate and copy others rather than think for themselves.

Losers are great talkers. They mouth generalizations and confuse activity with progress. They are complacent, secretive and defensive.

They try to do everything themselves and they resist new and external ideas.

Losers train by sheep dipping. Individual needs are not addressed. Immediate priorities take precedence over longer-term aims. A combination of attitudes, approaches and priorities locks change losers into a negative spiral of decline towards commodity product supplier status.

Winners in the challenge to change, transform and re-invent are very different. They recognize that change can be stressful and can disrupt valued relationships. They only alter what they need to change. Those affected are told why change is necessary.

Winners have a longer-term perspective. They become trusted business partners by enhancing their capabilities, deepening relationships, developing additional options and remaining relevant.

Winners are confident, positive and pro-active. They articulate compelling and distinctive visions. They build and release talent. They equip their people to make whatever changes need to be brought about.

Winners explore, pioneer and discover. They encourage enterprise and innovation. They trust other people, and share information and opportunities with them where this is likely to prove mutually beneficial.

Winners address the specific realities and practicalities of what they need to do to manage change. They inspire and motivate. They avoid wasted effort and concentrate upon the areas of greatest opportunity. They understand their customers and put themselves out to develop tailored responses to their requirements and bespoke offerings.

While open to ideas, winners select people, business partners and opportunities with care. They are persistent but pragmatic, and determined but adaptable in pursuit of their aims. They take calculated risks, experiment with new ways of working and learning, and create new knowledge, options and choices.

Winners value relationships. They empathise and invite feedback. They question and challenge, and listen and learn. They collaborate with complementary spirits who share their vision and values. They enter into partnering arrangements based upon openness and transparency.

The boards of change winners are competent and confident. They avoid the distractions of trappings. Their game is to inspire, enable and support growth, development and transformation. They cut through blather and hype to get down to the fundamentals of what needs to be done.

Winners prefer simple solutions and direct action. They think before they act, push back the boundaries of what is possible and become sought-after business partners. Effective change managers avoid diversions, panaceas and single solutions. They focus on activities that deliver the results they seek.

Change, renewal and transformation should be regarded as normal activities. Work with colleagues to foster winning attitudes and behaviours, and ensure a balance between change strategy and capability. All the pieces of the jigsaw puzzle required for successful transformation and sustained competitiveness should be in place.

Check that colleagues are clear about what they are trying to achieve and are visibly committed to agreed objectives. Make sure that people understand what they need to do and are enabled to act. Ensure barriers to change are identified and tackled. Problems will arise. Their absence could indicate a lack of ambition. Learning from them and celebrating success help to sustain momentum.

Further Information

*'Transforming the Company, Manage Change, Compete and Win' (2002) by Colin Coulson-Thomas, published by Kogan Page.

Chapter 14

CORPORATE COMMUNICATIONS

Work undertaken within the winning companies, winning people research programme has included different aspects of communications, for example within teams and across national borders. An initial communicating for change survey covered 52 organisations with a combined turnover of some £90 billion and employing 1.2 million people. Over a half of those participating were directors of their organisations, while a third held the job titles of chairman, chief executive or managing director. Other surveys have examined communication skills, and the role of communications within the boardroom and when winning new business and building relationships with customers.

Modern corporations are essentially networks of relationships based upon trust. When a reputation for fair dealing and accurate reporting is compromised, the consequences can be dramatic. Worldcom imploded.

Executives at Enron went to great lengths to conceal the true state of their companies' affairs. As a consequence, employees have forfeited their jobs and investors their savings. Association with misrepresentation sealed the fate of Arthur Andersen.

Are recent high profile scandals isolated instances of deception? Or is there a wider crisis in corporate communications? What lessons can be learned by boards of ambitious and growing companies who are eager to avoid the public fate of corporate failures? What do the winners do differently?

In this chapter we turn our attention to corporate communications. Corporate value statements advocate openness. Professional codes of practice champion integrity. Managers are expected to have 'communication skills'. Substantial investments have been made in communications processes and technologies. Communicating a distinctive vision, stretching goals and clear objectives can inspire, excite and energise people. However, many companies fall short of these ideals.

Looking at what communicators actually do rather than what they say reveals a wide gulf between corporate rhetoric and commercial reality. People are drowning in irrelevant information. They are over-loaded, overworked and insecure. With little time to think, many do not see the wood for the trees. Some suspect that corporate communications are all smoke and mirrors.

The author's research programme (see Introduction, page xv) has examined the communications practices of a wide range of companies in key areas such as winning business, building relationships and managing change*. Research teams compare the approaches of 'winners', companies that cope with changing circumstances, with 'losers', businesses that struggle or fail. Fundamental differences of attitudes and behaviour emerge.

Let's start with vulnerable companies and practices that should trigger alarm bells. Communications are largely top down and one-way. Communicators simply pass on whatever messages their bosses wish to communicate. They don't question a brief or ask whether information they are handed is accurate or fair.

Losers only communicate when *they* feel they need to. They become preoccupied with messages they would like to put across. Recipients are just targets. Smart communicators in floundering companies pride themselves on their ability to distract, exaggerate or keep a situation under wraps. They avoid speaking to people directly and hide behind technology. Sanitised summaries are posted on corporate Intranets.

The communications of struggling companies are often bland and non-committal. They give little away. Bad news is hidden under the carpet. Slick packaging encourages passive acceptance. Communicators mouth generalisations and repeat slogans. Their work is often of a high technical standard. But the focus is upon form and style rather than relevance and impact.

Communicators in stagnant and dying companies are emotionally detached. They display little personal commitment to corporate messages. Their communications are cold, clinical and bland. Many are sophists and cynics. Communications is a game to be played. Scoring points is more important than helping others to understand.

In ailing companies corporate communications is a distinct activity undertaken by dedicated specialists. They do the CEO's bidding, work mechanically and struggle to highlight what is different, special or unique about their employer. Not surprisingly they fail to connect with key stakeholder groups and spend much of their time rationalising failure. When they stumble, few help. People who have been tricked or feel duped look the other way.

Communicators in successful businesses are more confident and have less to hide. They behave very differently. They share information, knowledge and understanding with people whose cooperation is needed to achieve corporate aspirations. They engage in two-way communication. They encourage, welcome and react to feedback.

Good communicators are not pre-occupied with themselves. They focus on the people they would like to establish, build and sustain relationships with. They try to understand, empathise with and reflect their aspirations, hopes and fears. They make direct and personal contact. They feel. They may stumble over the words, but they demonstrate they care.

Communicators in winning companies consciously build mutually beneficial relationships. They forge longer-term partnerships. They are both sensitive and flexible. They listen. They monitor reactions and are alert to changing requirements. Communications activities evolve, as changes are made to ensure greater relevance.

Effective communicators identify unmet needs, analyse communications barriers and address problems. They recognise the importance of symbols and are visibly committed. They understand they and their colleagues will be judged by their actions and conduct. They endeavour to match words with deeds.

In companies with prospects communication is an integral element of management. It is built into work processes and the roles of managers. Communicators think for themselves. They question motivations, probe sources and assess likely implications. They take steps to ensure the veracity of corporate messages. They assume responsibility for what they communicate.

Winners explain with conviction the essence of what they are about. Their communications celebrate and sustain success. They engender allegiance and foster relationships that withstand market shocks and survive the traumas of economic downturn. People trust them and will put themselves out for them.

Investors, employees, customers, suppliers and independent directors should never take corporate communications for granted. The intelligence, standing and bravado of corporate leaders and their professional advisers are no guarantee the full story is being told. Be alert to tell-tale signs of whether communication approaches and practices indicate likely failure or herald future success.

Further Information

* Findings relating to effective communication are summarized in 'Transforming the Company, Manage Change, Compete and Win' (2002) by Colin Coulson-Thomas, available from Kogan Page.

Lessons of the research for communication with customers and prospects are summarised in 'Developing Strategic Customers & Key Accounts', 'Winning New Business, the critical success factors', the 'Close to the Customer' series of briefings and other titles in the 'winning business' series of reports which can be obtained from Policy Publications.

CHAPTER 15

GOING GLOBAL

HOW TO OPERATE EFFECTIVELY IN THE INTERNATIONAL MARKETPLACE

Aspects of going global have been explored by a number of the surveys undertaken within the winning companies, winning people research programme. For example, a European investigation of the human resources required for effective international operation involved 91 organisations employing over 2.7 million employees and with a combined turnover of some £320 billion. Of the survey respondents 38 per cent were chairmen, chief executives or managing directors. Field work with particular organisations has included projects with organisations in North and South America, Europe, Africa, the Middle East and Asia.

The horizons of ambitious managers today embrace the globe. Deregulation, privatization and market forces have eroded trade barriers. Budget airlines have reduced travel costs. The end of the cold war has created new opportunities.

Work can follow daylight around the globe allowing 24-hour-a-day operation. Resources can be accessed and activity undertaken locally, regionally or at global level depending upon requirements and comparative costs. Even sole traders use websites and email to make direct contact with customers all over the world.

However, operating in the international business environment also presents new challenges. There are commercial, legal and financial risks to consider. There are obstacles of distance, culture and time to overcome. In this chapter we will examine how to operate effectively in the international marketplace.

A continuing investigation led by the author (see Introduction, page xv) has examined the differing approaches of successful international operators and businesses that find it hard going. Comparing them reveals some lessons for those with aspirations to go global* – 'dos' that successful operators or winners practice and 'don'ts' that trip up losers.

Thinking global is the first step towards acting global. To take it you need to be aware of what is happening abroad. When you touch down, be open to new influences and receptive to alternative ideas. Winners are intuitive, perceptive and observant.

Retain a sense of perspective. Business people around the world can watch the news on cable television and receive regular feeds of stories that interest them direct to their desktops. Global media shape their attitudes and perceptions. But even MTV has its regional offerings, and requirements for products can vary greatly between national markets. The significance of borders will depend upon the business you are in,

Don't be overawed by the claims of others. Many so-called international companies are national enterprises that trade internationally. People who travel a lot sometimes hold onto stereotyped views or exaggerate national characteristics. Living and working abroad can reinforce existing prejudices. Some make an effort to adjust and adapt. Losers don't.

Appearances can be deceptive. A German manager who might seem formal and detached may contribute as much as a more voluble American. Reluctant Britons might observe a consensus outcome while delightful French colleagues may refuse to implement decisions they disagree with.

Many losers name drop and like to appear as citizens of the world. However, knowledge of the best bars in Amsterdam, Barcelona or Venice does not distinguish an 'international manager'. Attitudes, approaches and perspectives do. Internationally-aware managers are alert to developments in the global business environment.

True internationalization requires more than an ability to speak foreign languages. Learn from winners. Respect other viewpoints. Be tolerant of national differences. Actively support cultural diversity. Seek opportunities for foreign travel. Participate in overseas exchanges and job swaps. Join international project groups, task forces and teams.

Companies, like countries, can have distinct cultures. Be sensitive to differences and similarities in national assumptions, attitudes, and motivations. Try to reconcile conflicting interests, while recognizing that particular local requirements create opportunities for bespoke offerings.

Customer segments may or may not coincide with national borders. Experienced international operators are intuitive and cross-culturally aware. Learn to handle diversity and relationships with overseas colleagues. Mutual expectations need to be realistic and compatible. Address practicalities such as whether the technologies of the various parties will connect.

People likely to be interested in what you have to offer may be widely scattered. Keeping opportunities to yourself, trusting no one and operating alone will stunt your growth. Form relationships with complementary collaborators in other countries.

Some managers have a distorted understanding of overseas situations and harbour naïve expectations of international initiatives. Be realistic. Think through the implications of what you are setting out to do. Anticipate likely consequences, consider probable outcomes and assess possible reactions. Be prepared to address potential problem areas.

Recognize fundamental national differences and match words and deeds. Don't advocate diversity and variety, and then insist upon common approaches. Don't impose standard solutions that are inappropriate in particular locations. Wherever possible, tailor your approach to local circumstances and individual requirements.

Aim to communicate with customers and prospects in ways that are acceptable to them. Use languages they understand. If your intention is to become an international rather than a European player, you may need to give greater priority to Spanish and Portuguese.

Some executives talk about internationalization but then make sure that all key positions are in the hands of 'home country' nationals. Diversity can be a spur to creativity. If you get the chance, recruit and develop a multinational cadre of managers. Ensure opportunities go to those who are best qualified for each role.

Try not to force internationalization down your colleagues' throats. Let it occur naturally and tackle problems as they arise. Don't sweep difficulties under the carpet or hope they will go away. Allow people to network. Let them forge whatever cross-border relationships will best enable them to achieve their objectives.

Do not foist a single corporate culture on employees, customers and suppliers regardless of differing local conditions and unfavourable circumstances. Match your management style to how people with whom you wish to develop closer relationships operate.

Before you set up joint ventures with overseas businesses, make sure you and your colleagues are equipped to manage them. Be prepared to devote time to making them work. Because of the effort involved select prospects with care. Learn from your mistakes, and from your customers, suppliers and business partners.

Don't be pre-occupied with yourself. Emulate winners. Focus on the people with whom you would like to establish, build and sustain relationships. Understand them. Empathize with them. Respond to their aspirations, hopes and fears.

Effective international relationships are based on trust and respect. Lasting partnerships depend upon compatible interests. Establish a shared vision, common values, joint goals and agreed objectives. Consciously create mutually beneficial arrangements. Monitor reactions and be alert to changing requirements. And finally, celebrate, enjoy and sustain success.

Further Information

* The findings relating to successful internationalization are summarized in: 'Transforming the Company, Manage Change, Compete and Win' (2002) by Colin Coulson-Thomas is available from Kogan Page.

CHAPTER 16

NEW WAYS OF WORKING

In addition to surveys of changing organisations specific studies of particular ways of working have been undertaken within the winning companies, winning people research programme. A pan-European investigation of teleworking involved over 100 organisations and the production of the 21 case studies that appear within one of the three reports within the 'Responsive Organisation' boxed set. Other studies have looked at areas such as teleworking, teleconferencing and telemedicine. New ways of working and tools to support them have been introduced into several organisations. A methodology for adopting teleworking that has been produced by the research team has been used by over 100 organisations.

People should be able to work at whatever time and place enables them to best harness their potential and be effective at whatever tasks they are undertaking. The right way of working for one role or activity might not be appropriate for another. In some cases 'being there' might be important while other work could be 'location independent'.

Those who follow the advice of the last chapter and 'go global' will encounter many different attitudes to work in various parts of the world. Over a decade ago IBM, ICL and Rank Xerox operated tele-commuting networks. 'Telecoms' companies like BT and Cable and Wireless and the European Commission introduced various initiatives to promote more flexible patterns of work such as teleworking. However, their adoption has been much slower than champions and early enthusiasts predicted. While corporate structures have undergone significant change, many traditional ways of working persist.

Too often processes are simplified or re-engineered without fundamentally changing how, where, when or with whom particular tasks are undertaken. Yet a pan-European project team led by the author has developed 'The Responsive Organisation'* framework and methodology for introducing new ways of working during the course of process improvement activities. Doing both at the same time can massively increase the success rate of business restructuring and yield significant benefits for both people and organisations.

In this chapter we look at how to succeed with new ways of working. Flexible operation is the key to the success of many entrepreneurial companies. Hazell Carr offers the services of professional actuaries who work from home. Training services are provided to the freelance knowledge workers, and checks are in place to monitor the quality of calculations resulting from the company's virtual model of operation. Working at night enables RS Communication Services staff to install phone lines in City Offices while their users are asleep or clubbing.

Virgin and easyJet have based their business strategies upon doing things differently. Small companies sometimes give a lead when it comes to adopting alternative ways of working. Although operating in a traditional sector, Swift Construction allows its people to work flexible hours and job-share.

Cisco Systems grew rapidly by providing products that allowed others to use the Internet and embrace ebusiness. New ways of working also create business opportunities for those who help to make it happen. Telework Systems products include software for tracking, monitoring and managing mobile and remote workers.

Too often the workplace is a constraint, an overhead cost and the cause of sick building syndrome rather than an enabler of creativity and flexibility. Offices should be designed to support a variety of relationships, behaviours and patterns of interaction. To encourage imaginative thinking there should be quiet spaces for personal reflection, and activity areas for brainstorming and other group sessions.

What do winners – the more successful companies – do differently in relation to new ways of working? To answer this question we will draw upon the experience of case study companies in the three-volume set of reports 'The Responsive Organisation' and related findings from the author's continuing research programme (see Introduction, page xv).* We will start with the approaches of losers before moving onto the winners.

Losers tend to stick with a particular and hierarchical model of operation. The structure is set out in organisation charts. There are probably job descriptions for most positions, and how the organisation operates is set out in a physical or electronic manual. Preparing these and understanding them takes time. Hence people are reluctant to make changes that might involve altering diagrams, updating files and reprinting documents.

Some people become complacent. They believe they have discovered or created a formula for continuing business success. They also swear by particular approaches and enshrine them in standard processes and procedures. The framework solidifies.

Many losers have a weakness for single solutions, panaceas and fads. They believe that this management approach, that technology or a particular consultant's methodology will provide an answer or solve their problems. While struggling to make a chosen course of action work, they fail to consider alternative options. They lock themselves in.

Employees who can be trusted to operate in approved ways and observe standard practice are promoted. After some time corporate structures, processes, systems and mind-sets become rigid and inflexible. Subject them to increasing stress and they first creak and groan and then snap.

Increase workloads and transaction flows and people in 'loser' organisations struggle to cope. Rather than operate in new ways or change processes, they endeavour to work harder, faster and for longer hours. They quickly become overloaded and break down. Work–life balance is an issue in these companies because people suffer additional pressures without enjoying any of the compensating benefits.

There are often alternative ways of achieving the same objective. Winning corporate cultures are more tolerant of uncertainty and diversity. Their people think in terms of flows rather than structures. They reflect. They are willing to question, review and consider alternatives. Fluid roles, flexible systems and adaptable processes enable these organisations to move in new directions as situations and circumstances change.

Winners avoid blind allies and dead ends. They do not take continuing success for granted and are always open to alternative ways of operating. They are less wedded to precedent and more likely to treat each case on its own merits. They are also willing to re-invent themselves and to learn and work in new ways as the occasion demands. Innovative responses and novel approaches are recognised and rewarded.

Bespoke products and services are offered. Processes and their supporting systems exist to support developing relationships with customers. Learning is built into them. They are updated as required, and individual tasks are handled in whatever ways are thought to be most appropriate. People endeavour to improve and build upon what has gone before rather than merely replicate previous responses.

On the whole, winners are pragmatic, catholic and wary of 'single solutions'. They assemble creative and practical combinations of whatever ways of working and learning and change elements they feel will enable them to achieve their purposes. They are always alert to the possibility of better alternatives and vary the factors selected to improve outcomes and cope with changing circumstances.

Attitudes, processes, systems and ways of working and learning are relatively robust and resistant to stress. Because they flex to accommodate changing conditions and circumstances they do not fall over when the going gets tough. Winners handle new challenges and opportunities by prioritising, adapting and securing flexible access to whatever additional resources are required.

A new way of working must be appropriate for the tasks to be performed and the people concerned. Tasks should be defined in terms of delivering a specified 'output' with fixed parameters of cost and time. Ideal flexible workers are those who are inner directed and able to apply their knowledge and skill independent of any particular location.

People likely to be involved in a new way of working – and those who work with them – need to be involved and prepared. Clear objectives and targets should be set and health, safety and security issues addressed. Voluntary programmes are far more likely to succeed than those that are imposed. Regular communications with those who are working flexibly are also highly conducive of success.

Further Information

*A framework and methodology exists for introducing new ways of working while restructuring ['The Responsive Organisation' a three volume set of reports covering methodology, a tool kit and case studies] and re-engineering supply chains using the enabling technologies of electronic commerce ['The Competitive Network']. Details from Policy

Publications: Tel. +44 (0)1733 361149; Email colinct@tiscali.co.uk; or from www.ntwkfirm.com/bookshop

Some findings relating to new ways of working are also presented in 'The Future of the Organisation' and 'Transforming the Company, Manage Change, Compete and Win'. Both are by Colin Coulson-Thomas and published by Kogan Page.

C H A P T E R   1 7

MANAGING VIRTUAL ORGANIZATIONS

Several studies within the winning companies, winning people research programme have been concerned with aspects of building and management of 'network' and virtual organisations, including investigations of virtual team work and the management of distributed teams and teleworkers. Enabling technologies were among the areas examined by one pan-European investigation, while work with support tools has included an exercise involving over 1,000 separate organisations. Interviews with 69 individuals responsible for education, training and development within their organisations suggest many companies may be overlooking key members of the peripheral workforce.

Organizations used to consist of people we employed working in buildings we owned. No longer. With outsourcing, teleworking and electronic commerce, the 'virtual organization' can embrace people who work in a diversity of ways in widely scattered locations, and collaborating through a variety of contractual arrangements. Continuing the theme of new ways of working we turn in this chapter to how such organizations should be managed.

Developing a business normally involves harnessing and applying collective capabilities to the process of value creation. We are spoiled for choice in terms of where, when, how and with whom to work and learn. There are so many options for securing personal inputs in terms of employment status, place and hours of work, nature and duration of relationships, etc. This is the age of the 'designer organization'.

Emerging technologies can overcome barriers of function, distance and time, to bring together networks of complementary partners. Virtual teams are held together by a common sense of purpose, shared visions, and compatible goals and beliefs. Competition is increasingly between consortia of cooperating organizations, rather than individual enterprises.

Virtual companies composed of 'members' or 'business partners' specializing according to capability and interest compete successfully with larger corporations. Electronic commerce technologies are democratizing opportunities. The internet allows international communication for the price of a local call. Relevant contacts around the world can be accessed in seconds. Global distribution networks can be built in weeks.

Individuals in remote villages producing craft goods can cooperate to provide store buyers with electronic ordering systems superior to those offered by major manufacturers. Virtual operation offers small enterprises flexibility and responsiveness which many larger corporations only dream of.

Being on-line is crucial. Not being connected in the relationship age is the equivalent of physical incarceration on a remote island. Entrepreneurs with business visions are no longer frustrated by lack of people, money, or technology. Required capabilities are contracted in, perhaps in return for an equity stake.

No previous generation has had so many options to earn, learn and buy at times and places, and through relationships, of choice. People move between websites like birds flitting from one water hole to another. When loyalty can be no longer assumed, commercial success may be fleeting. Those who are absolutely outstanding are sought out. The merely very good are ignored.

Virtual operation raises many questions. How stable are relationships? How does one distinguish individual contributions? What are the risks of fraud, etc.? These and many other questions have been asked in an extensive examination of 'The Future of the Organization'*.

The management of virtual organizations – collaborators and contractors held together by electronic links, and by shared objectives and values – presents new challenges. It demands new sensitivities and new skills. Their governance – involving relationships with peers rather than subordinates – may require new people, personalities and practices in the boardroom.

Unsuccessful adopters – or losers – fail to anticipate the consequences of their actions. Wrong choices are made when 'non core competencies' are outsourced. Strategically important knowledge can be 'given away'; windows of opportunity can be missed. Management teams may find they have forgone the capability to respond to changing situations. Cutting out capabilities not directly related to immediate priorities may reduce the capacity to operate in tomorrow's markets.

When distinct areas of activity are contracted out to various organizations on differing timescales, both the discretion to flexibly re-deploy elements of a total capability and 'understanding of the whole' may be lost. Excessive fragmentation makes it more difficult for core values and goals to be shared.

Those forming a virtual organization should agree a common purpose and observe a framework of shared values and rules that will enable them to reap greater benefits from cooperative activities. What a network stands for and is seeking to do, will attract or repel potential members.

Successful adopters – or winners – recognize that self-awareness and honesty make it easier for people to play to their strengths and work cooperatively with others who have complementary capabilities. People need to be encouraged to discover their working and learning preferences.

Experienced learning or transformation partners can advise on the combinations of approaches, processes, technologies and patterns of work which are most appropriate for a particular company and provide counselling, mentoring and facilitation support specifically related to virtual collaboration (see www.ntwkfirm.com). Successful transition to virtual operation requires individual as well as corporate transformation. People may need to acquire networking, relationship and virtual team-building skills.

Virtual organizations, with their multiple relationships and on-line links, are particularly at risk of being intellectually asset stripped. Network security is critical. Many 'loser' boards act to safeguard physical and financial resources, while overlooking risks to intellectual property.

Winners understand that freedom encourages creativity. Thus measures to protect know-how should not stifle its development. The well of knowledge needs to be replenished. Parasites feed upon the supply, leaving renewal to others. It is important to monitor who is contributing to the virtual company and who is 'living off' it.

Information and knowledge can become commodities. When it is 'on the web', and easily and widely accessible, less value is put on knowledge for its own sake. To be harnessed and applied, information, understanding and expertise must relate to the purpose and objectives of an enterprise.

Shared commitment to learning is especially important. It attracts quality members, while the competitive positioning of a whole value chain could be undermined by the failure of particular collaborators to keep up to date. Adherence to certain principles, or signing a formal agreement covering network security, protection of intellectual property, and learning could be a condition of joining a virtual community.

The defeat of corporate giants by virtual SMEs is not inevitable. An EU framework exists for introducing new ways of working while restructuring ['The Responsive Organization'] and re-engineering supply chains using the enabling technologies of electronic commerce ['The Competitive Network'].* Texas Instruments, Jaguar, Motorola and other companies have built virtual networks that embrace both internal teams and external supply chain partners.

In an uncertain world, continuing relevance requires loyalty, learning and change. To quote from 'The Future of the Organization'* effective management of virtual organizations begins with people: 'listening, building relationships and understanding what is important and represents value and opportunity for them. ... It should be about empathy, flows, openness, trust and tolerance ... Success requires the matching of individual qualities, competencies, experience and motivation with a corporate environment that provides purpose, resources, commitment and support. Either without the other is likely to lead to frustration'.

Further Information

*Further information on 'The Responsive Organisation' and 'The Competitive Network' methodologies for introducing new ways of working and re-engineering supply chains respectively can be obtained from Policy Publications.

'The Future of the Organisation: Achieving Excellence through Business Transformation' by Colin Coulson-Thomas is published by Kogan Page.

CHAPTER 18

CREATING AN ENTREPRENEURIAL CULTURE

Studies of bidding and other ways of winning new business, the exploitation of know-how, and activities such as pricing and purchasing within the winning companies, winning people research programme have revealed a lack of innovation and creativity within many companies. Business development projects have been undertaken for over 100 organisations, and many of these have involved specific activity to build a more entrepreneurial corporate culture. Over 60 entrepreneurs participated in one exercise to develop more entrepreneurial approaches.

A corporate culture as well as an organisation's ways of working may need to be changed. Companies need to become enterprise colonies that tap, build, and release the entrepreneurial potential within their people and relevant external networks and communities. Ambitious individuals want to work with organisations rather than for them.

Designers of organisations, processes and systems face a dilemma. The standardisation of steps and responses can result in simplification and cost reduction. Induction becomes easier and results more predictable. Yet if taken too far, standardisation can result in commoditisation. Differentiation and bespoke responses may enable a premium price to be charged. Also talented people are demanding more discretion. They have an unprecedented range of choice in relation to how, when, where, for whom and with whom they work.

Increasingly, the challenge for companies is to attract potential entrepreneurs and business partners rather than dependent employees. More knowledge workers seek to live life on their own terms. Rather than approach organisations looking for work, ambitious, creative and confident individuals will treat corporations and colleagues as actual or potential collaborators. When comparing attitudes and approaches, there will no longer be such a stark divide between start-up enterprises and established businesses. Entrepreneurship, either alone or with corporate support, will be for the many rather than the few.

Companies will need to become more like incubators and enablers of new enterprises. New approaches and processes for the encouragement of entrepreneurship are required. Individuals and teams should be asked to come forward with new business ideas and ask for venture capital support, access to central services, and development and marketing assistance. A growing number of internal employees will emulate potential external partners by also seeking a share of the rewards for successful intrapreneurship.

An extensive examination led by the author has identified key requirements for 'shaping things to come' and achieving both commercial success and personal fulfilment*. People need to consider what they would really like to do and are especially good at as well as what potential customers would most like to have. Many smart people get paid to do the things they love to do. Some turn their hobbies into money-making ventures.

Once a business concept and potential customers have been identified the next steps are daunting ones for many would-be entrepreneurs. Securing initial funding, finding premises, recruiting staff and 'doing the books' can be time consuming and frustrating for those who would prefer to do other things. This is where collaboration with an established company can help. Yet, too many corporations are bureaucratic and ill-equipped to handle new ventures. The emphasis is upon 'consolidation' and sticking to 'core competences'.

As a consequence, many intending entrepreneurs do not think of taking their new business ideas to an existing employer or a local company operating in a related field or with complementary interests. Instead they look elsewhere for support. Maybe they are worried about losing control or feel that a big corporation might not be interested in a new venture.

Attitudes towards entrepreneurship within larger organisations are changing. But much more effort still needs to be devoted to creating more entrepreneurial cultures. Too often, restructuring, retrenchment and re-engineering are essentially negative activities concerned with survival not growth. The mood in some boardrooms is swinging against downsizing in favour of creating greater value for customers and generating additional income streams.

Many people are fed up with the defensive cost cutting practised by unsuccessful companies – or losers – and tired of being asked to do more with less. Many would like to change direction, reduce their dependency upon others, and lead more balanced lives. Employees used to seek security and a regular income. They undertook repetitive tasks, implemented standard procedures and followed prescribed rules. Today many want more than material rewards. They also want to build, develop and grow.

Customers too are restless. They demand distinctive and bespoke responses that reflect their individual concerns and priorities. People in client-facing roles are expected to behave more imaginatively when creating offerings to meet particular requirements.

Market leadership in key sectors will go to winners who innovate, or assemble a novel combination of elements that represents greater value for particular groups of consumers. Rather than refer to manuals, mechanically apply a methodology or provide standard offerings, people have to make choices and take risks. They are required to consider alternatives, and manage resources and expectations. In short, they must think and act like entrepreneurs.

Many existing employees are struggling to make the transition from corporate-dependent to intrapreneur and business partner. More companies are likely to recognise that they need external help and that some independent operators of smaller businesses may have the attitudes, skills and experience they require. Of course 'independants' are used to the freedom of operating alone. A clash of cultures could but might not arise as more big company bosses come to understand the requirements for contemporary market success.

Winners are more willing to empower responsibly. Giving individuals the discretion to do what they feel is most appropriate for each customer enables them to play a much more creative role. Their 'solutions' might contain unusual elements, unique features, novel approaches or new knowledge, which could be licensed to others. Opportunities abound for entrepreneurship and innovation in many walks of life.

The rapid adoption of *e*-Business is eroding barriers to entry. The imaginative can offer new ways of working, learning and earning that better match the preferences of those involved, and greatly increase the prospect of them achieving the twin goals of commercial success and personal fulfilment. This desired combination is most likely where personal and corporate aspirations are explicit, aligned and focused upon winning new business, establishing partnerships and benefiting customers.

Independent entrepreneurs and aspiring intrapreneurs will choose corporate patrons, partners and sponsors with care. For example, how much of the training budget is devoted to building entrepreneurial skills and supporting business development? They will consider whether a corporate culture and working environment encourages initiative, innovation and enterprise or stifles them.

Contracts, facilities, processes and systems should allow and enable questioning, resourceful and inventive individuals and business partners to explore and create. The rewards of successful innovation and entrepreneurship should be fairly allocated in proportion to the respective contributions of those involved. Separate incorporation of new ventures allows more people to become directors.

Intending entrepreneurs should seek out winners – flexible organisations that are tolerant of diversity and allow and enable people to be true to themselves and to play to their distinct strengths. Enterprise flourishes where people are enabled to work, learn and collaborate in ways that best enable them to harness their particular talents, and assemble new venture teams composed of individuals with compatible aspirations and complementary skills.

Confident people will join – and ambitious businesses will seek to work with – organisations that promote enterprise, support intrapreneurship and collaboration, and view them as potential business partners with ideas for new and profitable ventures. Arrangements should be in place to assess their proposals and provide concept development support and venture capital. Practical advice on securing family support, assembling a venture team and winning business should be provided, along with counselling on overcoming inhibitions, pitfalls and constraints, and getting started.

Farsighted companies will approach independent entrepreneurs when lining up the external support required by new ventures. Their internal procedures, processes and contractual arrangements will reflect the distinct and diverse needs of growing businesses. Their reward mechanisms will allow those responsible to participate in resulting financial returns.

Share-ownership, option or profit-sharing schemes may need to be established, to satisfy the increasing desire of individuals to build capital. Energetic and talented individuals who create knowledge rather than merely consume it, and who can innovate and develop tailored solutions, are seeking a greater share of the value that they create.

Investors should avoid losers – companies that do not champion enterprise and entrepreneurship. Their most capable people and most valuable customers will simply walk, and they will not attract the external partners they will require. Companies cannot afford to be excluded from successful new ventures established by independent entrepreneurs and past employees.

The interests of customers, independent entrepreneurs, companies and investors are rapidly converging. We are at a turning point in the relationship between people and organisations and between microbusinesses and larger companies. We have an historic opportunity to reconcile and align individual and corporate goals. If you are a corporate manager, go for it.

Further information

*'Individuals and Enterprise: creating entrepreneurs for the new millennium through personal transformation' and 'Shaping Things to Come, strategies for creating alternative enterprises' are published by Blackhall Publishing.

CHAPTER 19

ENTREPRENEURIAL PURCHASING

A total of 296 companies participated in the effective purchasing study which was supported by the European Institute of Purchasing Management. While the pan European survey covered a range of company sizes 44 per cent had a turnover of over one billion Euros and 43 per cent employed over 5,000 people. Business sectors in which purchasing can represent a particularly significant proportion of costs such as food and catering, IT and electronics, machinery and transport equipment, healthcare and pharmaceuticals were well represented in the survey. Purchasing processes have also been examined during projects with particular companies, including those with over 60 owner managers of SMEs.

'You are what you eat' is a slogan of our time. The corporate equivalent could arguably be 'you are what you buy'. While over indulgent eating can lead to obesity, flabby buying can drain a company's coffers and impair its performance.

In this chapter we shift our attention from sales to spending. The cash generated by a business is the difference between payments into and out of corporate bank accounts. Companies need to be entrepreneurial when buying from their suppliers as well as entrepreneurial when generating revenues from their customers.

Far too many purchasing teams focus on short-term issues and do not contribute to the formulation of corporate strategy or the development of new products. They fail to strike up and sustain relationships with external suppliers that might both help them to control costs and improve the quality of their offerings.

Many purchasing professionals also fail to secure senior management appointments because they struggle to demonstrate the value they are adding. They are perceived as paper processors rather than creative entrepreneurs. The attitudes, competences and approaches of many purchasing professionals need to change.

One of the research teams led by the author found that for almost 70% of the 296 companies surveyed purchases of external products or services amounted to over a half of their total costs, while all companies reported that their purchasing achievements were falling short of their aspirations. Clearly more effective purchasing can have a very significant impact upon the bottom line.

The 'effective purchasing' study of European purchasing was undertaken with the cooperation of the European Institute of Purchasing Management. The resulting 'Effective Purchasing, the Critical Success Factors' report* reveals significant differences between the approaches of winners and losers, the companies that succeed and fail respectively at achieving the benefits of effective purchasing.

Losers tend to view purchasing as an administrative activity of relatively low status that is sometimes a source of both management and quality problems. Purchasing arrangements are often fragmented, and attempts to consolidate them are viewed as empire building by cynical business colleagues. Targets tend to focus upon year on year savings, yet often ignore price movements over business cycles.

Purchases by losers are often ad hoc. Losers like to shop around. They avoid 'getting involved' with particular suppliers. They look for 'deals' and opportunities to make quick savings. They also fail to recognize differences of capabilities among different suppliers, and that one's approach to purchasing may need to vary according to factors such as degree of commoditization, volume, storage, transportation, quality and item importance, value or visibility to end customers.

Compared with effective purchasers losers are less successful at all of the considerations relating to choosing suppliers that were examined by the research team. Sometimes they have so many relationships with different suppliers to maintain that finding the time to assess individual providers and properly distinguish between alternative suppliers becomes difficult, if not impossible.

When negotiating losers play win-loose games. They keep their various suppliers at arms length and endeavour to play one supplier off against another. They tend to be oblivious to the longer-term consequences of their relentless drive to cut costs. The benefits of con-solidation, bulk-buying and cooperation elude them.

Losers give a low priority to the ethical employment, environmental and safety records of suppliers. They also seek to avoid the scrutiny of their colleagues, and are slow to assess their own performance. Winners are different. They measure and report their achievements, and demon-strate their contributions to colleagues. Their greater openness encour-ages others to have more confidence in them.

For winners purchasing is a source of competitive advantage. They work with their suppliers to reduce costs, innovate, improve quality or speed up deliveries. Involving purchasing and preferred suppliers ear-lier in the new product development process can often reduce the time required to bring new products to market by a quarter or more.

Winners are more likely to be involved in boardroom discussions of business strategy and new product development. Integrated systems are also more likely, that provide group-wide information and monitoring capability. Winners are able to show they are in control and achieving purchasing objectives. Their targets are more likely to include the build-ing of longer-term and partnering relationships with strategic suppliers, and integrating purchasing into group strategy.

In comparison with their less successful peers, winners are also more likely to pursue win-win approaches to negotiations. They recognize that building value can be as important as controlling costs, and that working with certain suppliers might enable the delivery of improve-ments and innovations that lead to more competitive offerings and ben-efits for both parties.

Canny winners recognize it is usually in their best interests that strategically important suppliers do well. Squeeze them too hard and they may lack the margins needed to fund the investments that would enable them to stay at the top of their game. Collaboration to find new ways of working together can lead to opportunities to save both sales costs for the supplier and purchasing costs for the customer.

Winners prefer longer-term contracts with reviews, and framework contracts with local call-offs. They are more interested in establishing and building collaborative relationships with a smaller number of strategic suppliers, and monitoring the quality of what is procured. They are also ahead when it comes to using IT and e-business technologies to automate aspects of purchasing, and facilitate methods of purchasing such as 'internet auctions'. Losers play catch up where the winners pioneer.

When assessing suppliers, winners look for a willingness to enter into a partnership, flexibility and senior management commitment. Other considerations when selecting key suppliers are product quality, low cost and delivery track-record, while for building a successful relationship responsiveness, technical support, technical leadership and – once again – flexibility are especially important.

In recent years purchasing has been transitioning from a regional to national and from national to multi-national model. In larger companies it is becoming increasingly continental or global in scope. Winners favour smaller but more able teams, made up of purchasing professional who endeavour to keep their skills up to date.

Losers appear to be some way behind the winners in relation to longer-term trends. Thus many of them were still centralizing, while their more successful peers who bought more centrally were devolving responsibilities to operating units within a framework of approved suppliers and group standards. Winners are more willing than losers to trust colleagues to make higher value purchases.

While losers buy a smaller proportion of a wider range of goods, winners are more likely to spend over half their total costs on bought in items. In particular, they enter into more partnership arrangements and are more willing to outsource. While the purchasing costs of losers are sometimes hidden, winners are both more aware of such costs and more likely to allocate them either to benefiting business units or central overheads.

Few companies appeared to have an integrated approach to checking the quality of purchased supplies. Winners were more likely to get the quality checking basics right, while losers tended to 'hope for the best'. Some losers play Russian roulette with quality, neither requiring supplier liability for faults, nor carrying out supplier audits.

Benefits of effective purchasing secured by purchasing winners include control of product quality, the integration of purchasing into group strategy and product plans, minimum costs of goods purchased, the use of standardized components/materials specifications, minimum work in progress stocks, security of supplies, partnerships with key suppliers, and retrospective discounts.

Losers tend to operate in isolation, while winners are more alert to what is happening in the marketplace. Effective purchasing teams aim to beat market prices by continually monitoring what others are buying, and taking immediate action to remedy any divergences of prices paid by competitors. Winners also embrace just-in-time or lean purchasing and benchmark their performance.

Companies with successful purchasing departments are more likely to be engaged in international trade. International sourcing is spreading and more activities are being outsourced, including the purchasing function itself. By adopting a more strategic approach, and acquiring the skills and experience to manage and monitor collaborative relationships, winners are more able to safeguard the intellectual capital and know-how needed for knowledge-based competitiveness.

It is important you understand where you are in relation to the differing approaches of winners and losers. The 'effective purchasing' database has been constructed to allow companies to benchmark their approaches against their peers in the survey sample and the winners who derive the most benefits from their purchasing functions. The fifteen page bespoke report* that is produced covers 137 purchasing issues and enables those who complete a questionnaire to identify the areas they most need to improve.

Further information

* 'Effective Purchasing, the critical success factors' and related bespoke benchmarking reports that compare corporate performance with the average for both all companies and those companies that win most benefits from their purchasing functions are available from Policy Publications.

CHAPTER 20

THE KNOWLEDGE ENTREPRENEUR

Studies of entrepreneurs and of information and knowledge entrepreneurship within the winning companies, winning people research programme have involved over 150 companies. A third of the participants have been CEOs of their organisations. The investigations reveal little effort to create and exploit intellectual capital and have been corroborated by other surveys undertaken by the programme team. For example, an interview survey covering 58 organisations revealed corporate learning activities to be focused upon the sharing of existing knowledge rather than the creation and exploitation of new know-how.

Many boards and management teams are missing exciting opportunities to transform corporate performance by better exploiting know-how and using job support tools to boost productivity. They are also forgoing unprecedented possibilities for generating additional revenues from new knowledge-based offerings.

Scientific breakthroughs occur in laboratories and innovative thinking abounds in workshops. Yet people drown in irrelevant information. They waste time and money on 'knowledge management' initiatives to capture and share existing know-how that may or may not be relevant to future aspirations. With unexploited intellectual capital all around them, executives imitate and copy others.

Companies are adopting managerial rather than entrepreneurial approaches. The focus is upon managing what is currently known, rather than creating new information and knowledge-based services, tools, ventures and businesses. Most knowledge management processes are missing an explicit knowledge exploitation stage.

Yet we stand at the threshold of a new management revolution. There is simply enormous potential for knowledge entrepreneurship, performance improvement and developing the additional knowledge needed to deliver greater customer and shareholder value. Continuing our theme of entrepreneurship we turn our attention in this chapter to the exploitation of know-how.

Most organisations and executives are barely scratching the surface. A recent investigation by the author* has examined processes and practices for exploiting knowledge. The findings highlight the scope for both improving the performance of existing operations and creating new knowledge-based products and services.

Whereas unsuccessful companies – or losers – were observed to be wasting resources by putting historic information of limited value on corporate Intranets, their more successful counterparts – or winners – were adopting a different approach. They were working with a combination of information, knowledge and tools to boost workgroup productivity and generate new income streams.

Winners understand that we need to step up from information management to knowledge entrepreneurship. There is an urgent requirement for knowledge entrepreneurs who know how to acquire, develop, package, share, manage and exploit information, knowledge and understanding and introduce related job support tools.

A new generation of practical support tools (see www.cotoco.com and chapter 24) incorporating critical success factors for competing and winning promise dramatic improvements in both understanding and achievement. The experiences of an A B C D E F of companies as varied as Avaya, B&Q, Cisco, Dana, Eyretel and Friends Provident suggest they represent the next 'big idea' in management.

These pioneers have used knowledge-based support tools to transform business win rates, launch new products and build supply chain quality. They can enable greater delegation and more bespoke responses in complex and regulated areas.

In relation to winning business, returns of over 20 times an initial investment have been quickly achieved. In addition to higher success rates, orders have been brought forward and dramatic reductions have been made in the number of specialist support staff required to accompany sales teams in the field.

Overall, much greater effort needs to be devoted to knowledge creation and exploitation. Directors and senior executives should assess the scope for knowledge entrepreneurship, and consider steps they might take to create and enable a community of knowledge entrepreneurs and stimulate and launch new knowledge-based ventures.

The extent to which the enormous potential of stored information and knowledge is realised, and additional revenues are generated, depends upon the energy and imagination of information and knowledge entrepreneurs, people whose calling and practice is the acquisition, development and commercial exploitation of information, knowledge and understanding. Let us look at the competencies required. The knowledge entrepreneur needs to understand how to:

- Acquire, develop, package, share, manage and exploit information, knowledge and understanding, and related support tools;
- Help and enable others to effectively use and apply them;
- Communicate and share information and complex knowledge in ways that assist comprehension and increase understanding;
- Create, badge, protect, manage and exploit intellectual capital and 'best practice' based job support tools;
- Identify and exploit market opportunities for distinctive information and knowledge based products and services;
- Develop and launch new information and knowledge based offerings and services;
- Use combinations of emerging technologies to network people, organisations and relevant sources of information, knowledge and support tools together;
- Handle knowledge in multiple formats, including animation, audio and video material;
- Develop and use appropriate job support tools to increase individual productivity and corporate performance;
- Collaborate with others, and work and learn in new ways in order to create and deliver greater value; and
- Lead and manage knowledge workers, network organisations and virtual teams.

Some knowledge entrepreneurs are instinctive. Others possess specialist expertise – for example, in corporate communications – or know about particular technologies. However, an overview appreciation of how people, know-how and technology can be brought together and beneficially managed, and also how to establish, launch and develop knowledge-based ventures are less widespread. They need to become more common if we are to grasp current opportunities to transform many aspects of our lives.

Individual business executives should aim to emulate winners by endeavouring to be role models when learning and sharing information, knowledge and understanding. They should understand the key requirements for success in the knowledge society and information age. Many boardroom and meeting room discussions would be enlightened by the presence of one or more knowledge entrepreneurs.

Many companies operate in sectors in which know-how accounts for an increasing proportion of the value being generated for customers. Yet they lack an explicit strategy for obtaining, developing, sharing and exploiting know-how. Corporate culture, policies, processes and practices should all be supportive of knowledge entrepreneurship.

Business executives need to ensure effective acquisition, development, sharing and exploitation of information, knowledge and understanding occurs within the areas for which they are responsible, and that their people are supported with appropriate knowledge based tools.

A designated person should be made personally accountable for corporate effectiveness at acquiring, creating, sharing and exploiting knowledge. Specific opportunities need to be assessed and important workgroups equipped with the support tools they need to do their jobs and achieve their objectives.

Just providing people with relevant knowledge may not be sufficient. They may also require tools to help them use and apply it. Practical knowledge-based tools can transform workgroup productivity by increasing understanding, communicating best practice and sharing the essence of how superstars operate.

There is little excuse for further inaction. 'The Knowledge Entrepreneur' provides lists of possible commercial ventures, along with detailed checklists for identifying and analysing opportunities, exercises for assessing entrepreneurial potential and 'scoping' possible knowledge-based services, and guidance on using support tools.

Further Information

*'The Knowledge Entrepreneur' (2003) by Colin Coulson-Thomas is published by Kogan Page.

CHAPTER 21

EXPLOITING CORPORATE KNOW-HOW

A total of 51 companies participated in the managing intellectual capital to grow shareholder value survey carried out in association with Financial Director magazine. The information collected was mainly provided by finance directors and financial controllers, but also by a number of managing directors, CEOs, company secretaries and business development directors. Company sizes ranged from less than £50 million (36.7%) to over £1 billion (12.2%). Aggregate revenues from exploiting the intellectual capital of the companies surveyed were in the region of £9.3 billion. This was more encouraging than the findings of another survey within the winning companies, winning people research programme covering 63 SMEs which revealed little effort to exploit intellectual capital.

Could you and your colleagues quickly secure new income streams and transform the productivity of your current operations by better exploiting what is already known? The most promising opportunities for revenue and profit growth are being overlooked in many companies. Processes for exploiting corporate know-how simply do not exist.

Many people ignore relatively easy ways of improving corporate performance and delivering greater shareholder value. They devote insufficient attention to the development, sharing and exploitation of information, knowledge and understanding.

They are also unaware of how relevant knowledge, critical success factors and the approaches of high performers can be built into work processes and support tools.

An investigation of the differing approaches of successful companies (winners) and their unsuccessful competitors (losers) has identified many opportunities for boosting profitability and generating additional revenue streams by better exploiting corporate know-how. The findings are set out in 'The Knowledge Entrepreneur'* a handbook with exercises for crafting new knowledge-based offerings and checklists of questions that individuals and boards need to ask to reveal the full extent of the possibilities.

In this chapter we will look at what the investigations tells us about the exploitation of corporate know-how – a core responsibility of the knowledge entrepreneur considered in the last chapter. Opportunities for income generation exist at all levels and in many areas of the companies examined. For example, thirty-one distinct learning support services were identified that a typical training and development unit could offer external customers.

The investigation reveals how a new generation of knowledge-based support tools can enable key workgroups such as new business and customer relations teams to adopt the approaches of superstars and emulate their behaviours. However, even the most successful of the companies examined are overlooking their existence and potential.

Corporate policies, systems and procedures are heavily biased towards physical assets and tangible activities. Considerable effort is devoted to protecting and maintaining physical assets, keeping records of them up-to-date, and ensuring they are properly depreciated and fairly valued in annual accounts, and physically verified by the auditors at the year end; while intellectual assets are inadequately managed.

Losers do little to capture, value and protect corporate know-how. In comparison, winners are more aware of how information flows, support tools, knowledge transfer, and the exchange and sharing of relevant understanding impact upon performance. They are more alert to the possibilities for knowledge entrepreneurship.

Reporting systems and performance indicators used by losers focus upon data that is easy to collect rather than the areas that are intrinsically of greatest importance. Few of them systematically assess, monitor and reward learning or the creation and exploitation of new intellectual capital. Many companies would benefit from tracking indicators such as net income from new knowledge-based ventures and offerings in relation to the value of available intellectual capital.

Winners are more aware of certain aspects of knowledge entrepreneurship such as fostering creativity or measuring and reporting intellectual capital. However, even among the more successful companies systematic strategies for creating and exploiting know-how across all functions and areas of operation were extremely rare.

The findings of the continuing investigation suggest certain key questions that need to be asked if entrepreneurs, boards and management teams are to create environments that are more conducive of knowledge entrepreneurship:

- Does the company operate in a sector in which know-how accounts for an increasing proportion of the value being generated for customers? If so, what are the implications?
- Do members of the board and management team understand the requirements for success in the knowledge society and information age? How many of them are knowledge entrepreneurs?
- Does the company have a convincing rationale and clear purpose? Is there a shared, distinctive and compelling vision? Does it reflect opportunities for knowledge entrepreneurship?
- Have the vision, mission, goals and objectives of the company been effectively communicated and shared? Have the various elements of capability – including relevant know-how – needed to achieve them been assembled?
- Is there an explicit strategy for the acquisition, development, sharing and exploitation of information, knowledge and understanding? Who has specific responsibility for it?
- Do people have the knowledge-based support tools they need to quickly communicate what is special and distinctive about the company and its offerings? Who ensures that important workgroups have the support tools they need to excel in their jobs?
- Are members of the board and management team role models in relation to learning and the sharing and exploitation of information, knowledge and understanding? Is the corporate culture – and are the attitudes, values and perspectives of the people of the organization – conducive of knowledge entrepreneurship?
- In particular, what action needs to be taken to break down barriers and overcome obstacles to the acquisition, development, sharing and exploitation of know-how?

- Is there effective two-way communication between the corporate centre and business units, and horizontal communication across functional, process and unit boundaries?
- Is the organisation moving up or sliding down the information, knowledge and understanding value chain within its sector of operation? Is priority given to the company's customers and the acquisition, development and application of the know-how needed to deliver more value to them?
- What explicit steps are being taken to create and support a community of knowledge entrepreneurs, create new knowledge based offerings and build practical support tools that make it easier for people to do their jobs and emulate the success of superstars?
- Have the key processes for the acquisition, development, sharing and exploitation of know-how been identified? Do information, knowledge and understanding flow effectively up, across and down the organization and around its networks of relationships?
- Are there opportunities for different individuals, work groups, business units, venture teams and business partners to develop ideas for new knowledge-based offerings and seek appropriate support? Are feedback loops built into the company's operating, learning and entrepreneurial processes? Are they regularly reviewed and refined?
- Finally, are the intellectual assets of the organization safeguarded as effectively as its financial and physical assets? How effectively and systematically are they being exploited? Is performance in these areas monitored?

The culture, policies, processes and practices of an organization should enable the effective acquisition, development, sharing and exploitation of know-how. Shrewd investors assess how effective companies are in these areas, and the extent to which people derive meaning and create opportunities, value and intellectual capital from various forms of information and knowledge. In essence they assess a board and management team's ability to encourage and enable knowledge entrepreneurship.

Further Information

*'The Knowledge Entrepreneur' (2003) by Colin Coulson-Thomas is published by Kogan Page.

How companies exploit 20 categories of intellectual capital is examined in the report 'Managing Intellectual Capital to Grow Shareholder Value' which is published by Policy Publications. The related title 'Developing a Corporate Learning Strategy' is also published by Policy Publications.

DEVELOPING A CORPORATE LEARNING STRATEGY

Aspects of corporate learning, including the development of directors generally and particular categories of director, the preparation of people for effective international operation and the development of bidding, project management and team working skills have been examined by different surveys within the winning companies, winning people research programme. The developing a corporate learning strategy survey involved interviews with 69 directors and managers with specific and corporate responsibility for the education, training and learning of more than 460,000 people. The 58 organisations covered had a combined turnover of over £49.5 billion.

Could your organisation and its people derive more benefit from training and development? Do they meet personal and professional development requirements and contribute to key business objectives such as winning new business? If all existing courses were closed down would customers notice or care?

Now is a good time to ask such questions. Training and development are at a watershed. Many existing courses and facilities are coming to the end of their useful lives. There are new approaches to learning and knowledge management to consider, emerging technologies to evaluate, and collaborative opportunities to assess.

Those responsible for corporate learning face tough choices and multiple challenges. Should a corporate university be set up? How might a corporate intranet best be used? Could business development and the processes of value and knowledge creation be better supported?

Certain options go to the heart of current operations. Should training and development be made a revenue centre or a distinct business? Could particular activities, or the whole function, be outsourced? What would be lost if 'central training' were closed down?

A two-year investigation by the author of corporate learning plans and priorities has examined these and other questions. It involved corporate visits and 69 structured interviews with those responsible for the training and development of some 460,000 people. The results, presented in the report 'Developing a Corporate Learning Strategy'* and summarized in this chapter, are sobering and demand urgent attention.

Many courses have passed their 'sell by' date. At the same time essential requirements and critical corporate priorities are being largely ignored. Too little effort is devoted to business development, relationship building, knowledge creation, e-business and entrepreneurship.

Overwhelmingly, the emphasis was upon squeezing costs, rather than the generation of incremental income streams. Only one of the organisations surveyed was equipping its people to be more successful at bidding for business, even though the top twenty bidding skills and critical success factors for winning bids have been identified and tried and tested bid management tools are available (see Appendix A and chapter 7).

Human resource teams are working hard, but many of them – particularly in struggling or 'loser' companies – do not appear to be connecting with the world around them. Millions have been spent on grandiose initiatives, fashionable concepts such as empowerment, and general 'quality', 'teamwork' and 'leadership' training, while particular requirements of critical importance are overlooked.

Critically, training inputs are not leading to new know-how and intellectual capital outputs. Existing understanding is being shared, but the new knowledge needed to compete and win and secure market leadership is not being created. Presentations on 'knowledge management' abound, but specific initiatives to develop knowledge entrepreneurs or equip people to use *e*-Business are few and far between.

The organisations examined focused overwhelmingly upon the internal development of employed staff. Customers, contractors, suppliers, associates and business partners – and external members of the supply chains and virtual organizations we considered in chapters 11 and 17 –

can all have development needs which could, and should, be addressed by shared learning.

Some of the more successful companies – or winners – have recognized that education, learning, training and updating are rapidly becoming global markets in their own rights. They are among the most exciting of contemporary business opportunities. However, in general training and development are not perceived as a source of incremental revenues. Nor are they used as a means of building relationships with key decision makers in strategic customers, suppliers and business partners.

Most losers among trainers appear to 'follow fashion'. Many buy 'off the shelf' rather than think about what would be most appropriate in specific situations. They provide standard programmes regardless of individual interests and needs. They expose people working on very different activities, to common experiences that have little relevance to their particular requirements and priorities.

Opportunities for training collaboration are also being missed. Many companies face similar development problems and challenges. Maybe the cost of new resources and facilities could be split between several users. There are also shared learning networks such as the Business Development Forum for those wanting to win more business.

Finally, the aspirations of individuals are often being overlooked. Trainers focus unashamedly upon corporate pre-occupations. Yet many people seek greater control and more balance in their lives. Switching the emphasis to innovation, entrepreneurship, and business building can enhance both corporate performance and personal fulfilment.

Not surprisingly, education, training and development expenditures are still sometimes viewed as a cost, rather than as strategic activities. They are not always considered vital investments in the creation of knowledge, intellectual capital and value for customers. There are exceptions. Glaxo Wellcome views innovation and creativity in the development of new products as a critical business process. Staff are helped to become more effective researchers.

All in all, the current state of affairs cannot continue. Those interviewed are sincere, hard working and personally committed to individual and corporate development. They derive little satisfaction from the situation revealed by the survey*.

So what needs to be done? Winners tend to be pioneers and innovators, rather than observers and imitators. They facilitate, enable and support development. They champion and reward learning and enterprise. Learning should be built into work processes and people's roles. It should embrace customers, suppliers and business partners.

Winners allow individuals to manage their own learning. They encourage their people to join shared learning networks and achieve breakthroughs in understanding. They establish corporate universities, foster learning partnerships, and keep their learning strategies current, relevant and vital. Standard offerings are abandoned in favour of specific and tailored interventions.

Training teams with the potential should be tasked with becoming profitable businesses in their own right. Training activities should contribute to enterprise, business and knowledge development. Providing individuals with personal learning accounts could create 'customers'.

Demonstrable outcomes should replace input indicators such as 'bums on seats'. For example, by how much has the 'win rate' in competitive bidding situations increased? What proportion of turnover do new products and services account for? What value is ascribed to new intellectual capital? Whenever a direct causal link to additional know-how, greater customer value or extra business cannot be demonstrated, activities should be discontinued.

'Human resource' professionals must work much more closely with their colleagues. Companies need to become incubators of entrepreneurial activity. Working environments should inspire and enable learning, innovation and creativity.

Many corporate learning strategies and practices need urgent review. Training teams are missing an historic opportunity to make a more strategic contribution to knowledge and value creation and the achievement of both personal and corporate objectives.

Further Information

* 'Developing a Corporate Learning Strategy' (1999) by Colin Coulson-Thomas is available from Policy Publications.

CHAPTER 23

MAXIMISING BENEFITS FROM IT AND E-BUSINESS

Within the winning companies, winning people research programme there have been specific surveys of the impact of particular technologies, including e-business and the IT director community. 56 different e-businesses were examined, while the competitive network methodology for re-engineering supply chains using e-business technologies was based upon an examination of over 40 re-engineering methodologies and a pan-European investigation. Innovative applications were encountered across a wide range of organisation sizes, different areas of business and the public sector.

Information technology (IT) and e-business should support how people would prefer to work and learn, and enable them to operate in new and better ways. But too often it constricts and constrains rather than liberates. Individuals and teams have to compromise and change in order to fit in with the requirements of technology. The successful operation of IT becomes an end in itself.

Poor investments in IT set existing ways of operating in concrete rather than creating additional options, value and choices for customers. IT should support more intimate relationships with customers, suppliers and business partners; facilitate learning, adaptation and change; enable entrepreneurship and integrate learning and working. It should make it easy for people to share information, knowledge and expertise. Smart users employ it to secure operating efficiencies and create new electronic markets.

So what do the winners do differently to make IT and e-Business an enabler rather than a barrier? To answer these questions a continuing research programme led by the author (see Introduction, page xv) has examined the corporate experience of over 2,000 companies. The results* are presented in a series of related titles (see Appendix B). This chapter summarises what companies should do to maximise the benefits of using IT and e-business.

The less successful or losers tend to adopt cautious, tentative and half-hearted approaches. They dabble and test rather than fully commit. For example, they may create static websites featuring background information about themselves and then use the lack of visitors that is likely to result as a vindication of the modest nature of their investment. The consequences of their lack of imagination and relative inaction are used to justify further lethargy and inertia.

When losers do act they are often naive and give little thought to the likely reactions of others. They decide they too would like a web presence and its establishment becomes an end in itself irrespective of whether it has a purpose or would help achieve certain objectives. Not surprisingly, the sites that result attract few visitors.

The more successful or winners are more positive, considered and open-minded. They use e-business to expand their customer base and provide additional support services to existing consumers. Some replace physical market places with new electronic market spaces.

People in winning companies get to know website visitors and their interests, and endeavour to provide a complete, personalised and regularly updated service or experience. They start with a problem or opportunity from a user perspective.

Winners think about how new e-business channels might make it easier for customers to access the information and opportunities that *they* need. They examine ways in which selection and purchasing might be made simpler for suppliers, for example by providing on-line search, configuration, pricing and cost-justification tools.

Every effort is made to build iterative relationships with each individual and provide additional value to that which might be obtained from any alternatives. Wherever possible visitors are enabled to help themselves. Electronic templates allow visitors to present their requirements, or any problems they might have, in a way that makes it easier to provide a relevant response. On-line services could range from simple ordering and tracking systems to complex self-design facilities.

Winners invite feedback from users and their people are encouraged to actively consider how they can make more extensive use of *e*-business applications. Reactions, comments and suggestions are sought, obtained and acted upon. The financial costs involved represent a minor element of the total investment of time and commitment in creating services and facilities that meet user needs and lock them in.

Winners create and actively participate in virtual communities. They encourage mutual sharing and support. By enabling interaction and introducing dynamic elements they encourage repeat visits. Regular reviews occur and findings are acted upon to help ensure that whatever is offered continues to be of interest, relevant and vital. Their involvement enables them to monitor trends, identify evolving concerns and spot emerging aspirations and requirements before they crystallise.

E-business technologies and principles are being used to create new markets and change how business is done. For example, procurement is undertaken electronically. Intelligent agents search for suitable suppliers. Opportunities are put out to electronic auction.

A company's web presence can be used in many ways to build closer and interactive relationships with customers. Many IT companies allow their software products to be purchased and downloaded via the Internet. Guinness produced a screen saver version of its Guinness.com website that can be downloaded.

Electronic links can encourage intimacy and enable 24-hour trading and access to information, knowledge and opportunities. Responses can be made within seconds. On-line visitors can be helped to diagnose problems, assess requirements and assemble or develop solutions. E-Business and mobile technologies are profoundly changing relationships between businesses and their customers, suppliers and business partners.

There are so many opportunities to challenge and improve on current practices that all members of staff should be encouraged to consider the possibilities. Ford in the US and Powergen in the UK have provided all their employees with a home computer. Senior managers believe the skills and experience they acquire will benefit their contributions during office hours.

Success can depend upon the extent to which a web presence is accessible, distinctive and memorable. Follow-up fulfilment processes and offerings need to be in place to ensure that after an initial contact interested visitors are converted into buyers and continuing relationships are forged.

Federal Express has redesigned its core business processes to allow the great bulk of its parcel shipments to be ordered, arranged and managed via the Internet. At any time during the day or night customers can log on and see exactly where each item is. The company's most valuable assets used to be its trucks and aeroplanes. Its value now primarily derives from its processes and supporting software.

The trick is to apply technology to the critical success factors for business success. Too many investments are in areas that do not make the difference between winning and losing. Standard packages may be fine for non-critical activities but bespoke development in crucial areas for competitive advantage can differentiate and result in the creation of new intellectual capital.

Intimate and mutually beneficial relationships are the key to bespoke responses and sustained knowledge and value creation. The effective use of IT has become very dependent upon attitudes towards such relationships, especially 'external' parties and customers in particular. The key question is the extent to which they are perceived and treated as full members or citizens of the network.

Further Information

*'The Competitive Network' report and methodology shows how to combine e-business with re-engineering to build value creating supply chains and win new markets. Details and information on the related 'The Responsive Organization' re-engineering methodology 'for introducing new ways of working can be obtained from Policy Publications.

Findings relating to the creation of a network form of organization are presented in 'Transforming the Company, Manage Change, Compete and Win' (2002) by Colin Coulson-Thomas and published by Kogan Page.

CHAPTER 24

BOOSTING WORKGROUP PERFORMANCE AND SALESFORCE PRODUCTIVITY

USING JOB SUPPORT TOOLS TO INCREASE SALES AND LAUNCH NEW PRODUCTS

In the last chapter we learned some general lessons about how to make the best use of IT. In this chapter we will examine a particular application area – using relevant knowledge and the approaches of high achievers to boost workgroup productivity.

Over 1,400 companies have participated in surveys within the winning companies, winning people research programme concerned with identifying critical success factors for particular corporate activities. Projects to incorporate critical success factors and the approaches of the more successful companies within these surveys into processes and support tools have been undertaken for financial services, engineering, manufacturing, retailing and telecommunications companies. Evaluation studies have confirmed the significant improvements in productivity that have been achieved.

A new generation of job support tools are transforming workgroup productivity and corporate performance. Let us look as some examples from an investigation of how to boost the performance of key workgroups such as sales and marketing teams*. As the number of pioneers in this field is still relatively small this particular chapter will include some quotations from those involved.

Your marketing plans look good on paper, but are people in the front line equipped to implement them? Sales support tools can help your people to get your message across and win more orders.

Many companies initiate grandiose knowledge management initiatives but do little to help staff improve their performance. Putting information on an Intranet is not enough. The expertise to do something better, new or different may require additional skills and tools, as well as access to relevant knowledge. Successful companies take practical steps to enable their people to compete and win.

Improved sales of existing products and more successful product launches are the ambition of every board. Practical knowledge-based job support tools can help achieve this aim. They can incorporate critical success factors and how high performers operate, capture and spread best practice and improve product and market knowledge.

Many sales teams are being pressured to win more orders. With competitors snapping at their heels and customers demanding more bespoke responses, prices and margins are under threat. No wonder sales staff turnover is sometimes so high.

While superstars achieve their targets, many average performers rely increasingly upon specialist support. Some ignore regulatory requirements, make errors when pricing, or leave out standard clauses from proposals. They struggle to explain what is special and distinctive about their offerings.

Eyretel whose products recorded and analysed telephone calls found its growth limited by the speed with which it could recruit, induct and train new sales representatives and bring existing staff up to speed with new offerings. According to Marketing Director, Nathan George: "We had to find a way to get knowledge about our sophisticated product line to a large number of sales people quickly".

Co*t*oco, a supplier of bespoke support tools, developed a laptop based toolkit with animations to explain Eyretel's voice recording solution, multimedia tours of its software, slide presentations, price and cost justification calculators and report generators. The result made such an impact on increasing sales and reducing sales costs that Eyretel won an eBusiness Innovation Award.

Sales support packages developed for 3Com, Cisco, Dana, ICB and The Innovation Group have included interactive presentations, demonstrations of products in operation, decision trees to assist account planning, and tools for developing and pricing solutions. Job support tools can use whatever formats – from text and graphics to animations, visual images and video and audio material – best help understanding.

Sales support tools are particularly suited to the launch of new products. A single repository like K-frame (www.k-frame.com) can hold all the information and knowledge needed. Technical details can be quickly communicated to groups in various locations around the world. Animations and video footage can be used to show offerings in use, and secrecy can be maintained until the moment of release.

The Innovation Group has used support tools to launch a new Local Authority operating system and roll out its project management methodology. 3Com has employed a similar tool to introduce network products to both direct and indirect channels.

A sales support package can gather together the critical information, knowledge and tools a sales person needs. It can incorporate 'best practice' and the approaches used by 'superstars' as well as key success factors for winning business identified by the winning business research programme led by the author. It can also ensure sales people focus on value and benefits to the customer rather than product features.

Even with complex products, tools can be used to assess customer requirements and configure solutions. Multimedia capabilities usually enhance the portrayal of corporate credentials and capabilities, while animations can bring technology to life.

ICB uses its 'Navigator' sales support tool to build product knowledge and communicate with customers. According to Marketing Director Janetta Evans "We now rely on the simple but effective tool as the knowledge base for the whole company. Navigator will become an intrinsic part of how ICB works."

Support tools can automate routine tasks and provide support for every stage of the sales process from prospecting and qualification to negotiation meetings. Commercial, quality and regulatory checks can be built in. A library of background information can help users to answer customers' questions on the spot. Marketing materials can include templates, case studies, testimonials and independent endorsements, competitor analysis, and industry and market knowledge.

Don Fuller of Cotoco emphasises: "Seamless links can be provided to websites and on-line applications. Feedback mechanisms can gather information from the field. Tools can help sales people identify cross-selling and upgrade opportunities."

Support tools can also ensure consistent application of best sales practice and a high standard of proposals. Marked improvements in product and market knowledge can occur. Other benefits include fewer errors, higher win rates, greater customer retention, less support staff, increased order value, and lower sale force churn.

Refining the sales process and making it easy for people to follow can increase sales. Better prospecting and improved qualification can focus effort on the most productive accounts. New staff can be inducted more quickly.

Prospects can use tools to discover new options that better meet their needs. When operating it themselves some customers order more than they would with a sales representative present. They feel in control and can explore alternatives in their own time. Automated calculations enable them to quickly assess the consequences of different approaches.

Sales support tools can be used to secure control over an indirect sales process. Consistent messages can be delivered to market. Training costs can be slashed by ensuring material is easy to learn and use, and instantly accessible. Reliance upon specialist staff can be reduced considerably.

Friends Provident uses a sales development support toolkit called THE MARKiT to assist staff running local marketing campaigns. Stuart Wilson, the company's Marketing Development Manager explains: "The business objective was to deliver an interactive toolkit that would help sales managers and their teams respond to requests for mailshots, local ads, posters and other lead generation material."

Support tools allow managers to maintain quality and avoid risks when delegating responsibilities. The automation of routine tasks frees up time for the greater differentiation and tailoring that may enable a price premium to be charged. Sometimes less experienced and qualified staff can be used.

Don Fuller, the Managing Director of Cotoco, believes: "Learning through doing is particularly effective. Building knowledge into tools makes it very easy for people to get complex tasks right first time and every time." Using them can be a differentiator. A systematic and customer focused approach enhances a supplier's reputation and helps to build relationships.

Companies should endeavour to avoid using tools that de-skill. According to Don Fuller"Support tools should help people to learn rapidly. They should improve understanding." Cisco's IP Telephony Sales Tool up-skills people working in its direct and indirect sales channels. As users work through prospect qualification and other tools, windows open up to explain why certain courses of action are advocated. They learn from each use.

Ease of use is critical to success. Stuart Wilson describes Friends Provident's requirement: "The toolkit had to be simple to use and capable of processing a large quantity of material in an interactive and user-friendly fashion, whilst also being flexible enough to cater for additional information to be added as required quickly and easily." According to Don Fuller: "To encourage take up and change behaviour support tools should provide the easiest way to accomplish desired outcomes."

For Stuart Wilson the impact of THE MARKiT toolkit "has been impressive. We are very pleased with the end result, having achieved and indeed exceeded our original expectations." Janetta Evans of ICB is another satisfied user: "The message, the confidence, the ability to prove what we sell as a deliverable have all been greatly enhanced – this must lead to a great return on investment."

Users of support tools report significant increases in productivity and the ease with which best practice can be spread. As mentioned in chapter 20, quick paybacks of the cost of developing them can be achieved. Returns on investment of 20:1 or more can be obtained – in one case over 100:1 on a single order.

However, the IT losers we examined in the last chapter should be on their guard. According to Ed Thompson, Research Director of Gartner, sales technology often fails to deliver: "Seventy five percent of sales application projects are perceived by their users to have failed to meet expectations twelve months after deployment."

Thompson believes that ill-considered sales technology can be bad for you, but as Eyretel found, new and less experienced sales staff can benefit enormously. The key is not trying to shave a few percent off administrative time, but in focusing on what happens in front of the customer.

Eyretel's tool helped both its own people and customers to better understand its technology and products. Users felt so confident in the presence of customers that the ratio of support to sales staff was cut by a third. Win rates increased, orders were brought forward and more professional presentations delivered. Eyretel's Founder Roger Keenan described the tool as "by far the most professional piece of marketing Eyretel has ever produced."

Gartner's research suggests the key to success is to improve a process before automating it. Don Fuller agrees: "Improvements based upon the insights of superstar sales people are more likely to get outstanding results than automating current practices." Content is critical. During development review existing approaches and incorporate useful short cuts and how high achievers operate.

Friends Provident considered paper-based guides. However Stuart Wilson and his colleagues: "recognised that these documents could very easily become shelf-fillers, gathering dust and rarely used. The company had a huge library of available materials. The challenge was finding how to present it in the most user-friendly way."

Successful users of IT or winners generally find that the best results with support tools are usually achieved with relatively homogenous groups of people undertaking similar tasks. They avoid fixed and inflexible tools in areas undergoing rapid change, unless arrangements are made for continuing review and regular updating. Don Fuller insists: "Ongoing maintenance can greatly increase a tool's shelf life."

Gartner's research found that successful projects need clear goals, management commitment, a sound process and sales force buy in. Stuart Wilson confirms that: "Close liaison between the field, our IT, compliance and design departments has been vital."

Too often sales tools focus on management's needs for reports rather than more effective selling and this approach can be disastrous. Ed Thompson explains: "Many companies never recover the impact of six months disruption while the new technology is being adopted". The focus becomes back office administration rather than performance in front of the customer.

"A sales support tool should focus unashamedly upon helping users land more business," argues Don Fuller. "The 80/20 rule is critical. Improve the 20% of the job role that delivers 80% of the business gain."

Once support requirements have been agreed, rapid progress can usually be made. Even complex tools can be developed and tested within a few weeks of a go ahead. Winners find that the introduction of a new tool needs to be carefully planned if people are to obtain the maximum of benefit from it. Putting a CD-ROM disc into the post is not enough. Make sure people understand the significance of what is provided.

Stuart Wilson has no doubt the effort of producing The MARKiT was worth it: "We now have a powerful and, within the Financial Services sector, a unique marketing support tool for our Sales management team."

Further Information:

*Job support tools are discussed in 'The Knowledge Entrepreneur' (2003) by Colin Coulson-Thomas and published by Kogan Page.

CHAPTER 25

WORKING WITH CONSULTANTS

In the last chapter we saw how specialist help is enabling pioneering companies to boost workgroup productivity. However, many business leaders have a love–hate relationship with consultants. While they may resent the high cost of 'external inputs', their slimmed down organisations are often more dependent than ever upon bought-in advice as a result of no longer carrying a 'float' of resources to cope with unforeseen events or major challenges.

Studies within the winning companies, winning people research programme concerning particular professional communities, change management and business development activities have examined the role of consultants. For example, the 91 participants in the survey covering preparation for international operation were asked about the contribution of consultants, while most of those involved in a study of project management managed teams of consultants. Over 150 consulting projects have been undertaken in the course of the programme, and particular surveys have been supported by groups of consultants, for example the Institute of Management Consultants and the Association of Consulting Engineers in the case of two of the winning new business studies.

Cynical consultants ingratiate themselves with chief executives, and encourage dependency by encouraging them to doubt the competence of their internal colleagues. Clients can end up paying large sums of money for 'projects' that do them little good, and sometimes cause great harm.

Many external consultants continually peddle new ideas to companies that would benefit from traditional remedies. Tesco has prospered at the expense of rivals by focusing unashamedly on the basics of

successful retailing, particularly the creation of greater value for customers, while at the same time moving into on-line shopping and expansion overseas.

Many companies attach excessive credence to the counsel of external
and uninvolved experts, while paying little attention to the views of
their customers. The Shell.com website provides discussion group facilities that allow the oil company to seek opinions from interested supporters whether they are allies or critics. Their responses can be taken
into account when policies are reviewed.

So what do successful companies or winners do differently from losers when working with consultants? This question is among those considered by the research and best practice programme led by the author
(see Introduction, page xv) which has examined the experience of over
2,000 companies. This chapter summarises what can be learned from the
findings* in relation to building beneficial relationships with
consultants.

Let's start with losers in struggling, stagnant and failing companies.
They sometimes use consultants because they lack the energy and intellectual rigour to themselves handle issues they are paid to confront.
Insecurity may also cause them to hire an outside party who can be
blamed if events do not turn out as planned.

Losers become dependants. They end up relying upon consultants to
tell them what to do and how to do it. They also take a short-term and
project view of relationships with consultants. There is little cross fertil-
isation and limited learning across and between individual projects.

Many losers are fixed in their views, or think they know best, even
though their performance may suggest otherwise. They are resistant to
new ideas and alternative courses of action, and are reluctant to learn
from outsiders.

Losers tend to fall back upon existing approaches and tried and
tested techniques. They adopt standard solutions, methodologies and
packages, and seek general improvements in performance rather than
the achievement of specific changes.

Rather than demand original and bespoke approaches that could
result in competitive advantage, losers employ consultants who work
systematically through their firm's methodology manuals and implement 'me-too' solutions. They also become lost in the intricacies of

complex mega-projects, and do not understand how the products and services of different suppliers interrelate with each other.

Losers focus upon what is immediately apparent. They do not search for underlying root causes. They are reluctant partners, and they fail to exploit the full potential of their know-how or prevent its gratis use by others, including rapacious consultants.

Winners who succeed in managing change, competing and becoming market leaders are different. They do not mind being challenged. When they seek external help it is not to avoid their responsibilities, but to obtain independent, objective and informed views from carefully chosen consultants with relevant experience and expertise.

Winners remain in control. They retain ownership of change programmes and do not abdicate this responsibility to external parties. They give consultants clear direction and seek specific help and longer-term and partnering relationships with those who share their objectives. They learn from and with external parties they respect.

Confident winners will try new approaches. They are prepared to develop their own methodologies and techniques. They also prefer to secure bespoke approaches to particular problems, and they endeavour to achieve specified outcomes. Deliverables are defined in clear output terms.

Winners are demanding customers, and ensure consultants get to grips with their particular issues and 'deliver'. They use consultants who understand what is at stake, and ensure they address what is unique and special about an individual company's situation and circumstances. They remain focused. They do not allow themselves to be bamboozled by consultants or sold additional services they do not need.

To ensure different elements of a solution are compatible, winners endeavour to understand how individual products and external services complement and work with each other. They also attempt to comprehend root causes and ensure consultants address underlying drivers rather than surface symptoms.

At the end of assignments, winners try to learn from what has happened in order to increase their internal capability to handle other similar situations. They may put 'knowledge transfer' into a consultancy contract and ensure that it occurs. They form mutually beneficial learning partnerships with advisors, consultants and business partners, and both manage and exploit the know-how that results.

Further Information

*'Transforming the Company, Manage Change, Compete and Win' (2002) and 'The Knowledge Entrepreneur' (2003) by Colin Coulson-Thomas are published by Kogan Page.

CHAPTER 26

USING MANAGEMENT METHODOLOGIES, TOOLS AND TECHNIQUES

Initial research concerned quality, with two surveys covering 205 organisations employing some four million people and with a combined turnover of £344.6 billion. Two thirds of the respondents were directors of their organisations, 71 of whom were chairmen or chief executives. Subsequent investigations have examined differing approaches to process improvement and re-engineering, business excellence and the use of emerging technologies and a new generation of job support tools. Specific project work has been undertaken in over 100 organisations. Three of these projects have been among the largest and most complex implementations undertaken during the years concerned.

Many organizations adopt a variety of management approaches, methodologies, tools and techniques for bringing about significant change. However, subsequent experience of their use suggests a considerable gap between expectations and outcomes when they are used in particular corporate contexts.

Many 'change management' and other approaches and techniques are products of particular sets of circumstances. How relevant are they to contemporary concerns? How could or should they be used to better effect?

These and related questions were explored during an extensive and international investigation of corporate transformation experience and practice (see Introduction, page xv). The results are summarized in 'The Future of the Organization: Achieving Excellence through Business Transformation'*.

In the last two chapters we examined the use of job support tools and consultants who are often the source of new management methodologies, tools and techniques. This chapter summarizes the research findings relating to how their offerings – and home grown equivalents – might be effectively adopted and deployed.

While widespread frustration was encountered, we may be closer to success than many have realised. But first we need to put an unhealthy obsession with standard approaches, tools and techniques to one side. They should be an aid to thinking, rather than a substitute for it. Careful selection according to relevance is essential. More thought is sometimes devoted to the choice of tool than to the selection of the problem to address.

Too many applications of existing approaches and tools, particularly in struggling organizations or losers, are concerned with working people harder or the depressing task of downsizing, rightsizing or reducing the organization to its 'core'. The roots of most of the original ideas behind the innovations examined in the course of preparing 'The Future of the Organization' generally lay outside of the world of work, when seeing a link or connection caused someone to ask a simple, yet fundamental, question. Instead of trapping their organizations within a descending spiral of cost-cutting and despair, their proponents focused upon opportunities and capabilities that could sustain a positive spiral of growth and development.

Those applying management tools tend to focus upon the more visible 'formal' factors. Thus processes are documented and re-engineered, and organization charts are redrawn to reflect the latest restructuring. The trickier 'behavioural' or 'informal' arena of attitudes, feelings and values, is often avoided. Changing the architecture of the corporation may have little impact upon its ethos, culture and soul.

The standard approaches adopted by many losers are dangerous when used as an alternative for careful thought about what would be best in a particular context. Too much attention is devoted to 'tried and tested' tools and existing approaches and activities. Identifying missing elements and devising and adopting new approaches may have greater relevance to bringing about what ought to be.

People in pioneer organizations make the transition from consumers to producers of management tools and techniques in order to address the distinctive features of their own situations and circumstances. At some point companies aspiring to market leadership develop new approaches rather than absorb, consume or improve existing approaches. Winners create rather than imitate.

We need the courage to formulate our own philosophies of business and develop our own tools and approaches. Inspiration should be sought from what is simple yet fundamental, and from within rather than from what is trendy. Proactive and flexible innovators and users initiate trends, fashions and opportunities. They have vision and purpose, and adopt pragmatic criteria for development and selection and adapt to changing requirements and contexts.

Too many people are still victims rather than beneficiaries of restructuring and re-engineering. They work ever harder rather than more effectively on the things which really matter. Losers often lack time for reflection. People who 'rush about' sometimes fail to stay in one place long enough to think issues through or make an impact. The Buddha evolved his philosophy by sitting under a tree and thinking. Individual and corporate self-awareness and self-knowledge can help each to establish what they are particularly good at.

Winners understand that it is what we apply management approaches to and for what ends that generally determines whether or not they bite us. The rationale of organizations should be to develop and harness the potential and capabilities of both individuals and teams, and to apply collective capability and commitment to those activities that deliver value to customers and achieve business objectives'. Thus 'BPR' could be undertaken to re-engineer learning processes to improve the quality of working life, introduce new ways of working or learning, widen job opportunities or help create a learning organization.

Tools that encourage learning and development are especially valuable. Shared learning approaches and tools can help to hold groups and networks together. Their refinement and development can become a key benefit of network membership.

Commitment to learning and change, with emphasis upon empathy, openness, trust and tolerance, and knowledge, capability, and competence can enable renewal and relevance in an uncertain, insecure and transient world. These are the very areas often most undermined by corporate change programmes.

Learning can be a critical core competence. The support of learning or transformation partners can help an organization identify and overcome barriers to learning. They can advise on appropriate learning approaches and technologies and generally help to assess and improve the quality of individual, group and organizational learning. Shared learning across functional, project group, business unit and organisational boundaries can be particularly beneficial.

Winners stress the fun of shared learning and future discovery rather than dwell on the frustration, disappointment and pain of past restructuring. People should be encouraged to work and learn in whatever ways suit their circumstances and preferences, match their aptitudes and allow them to give of their best. Social creatures thrive on trust, and the interaction and interdependence that allow individuals to create and negotiate roles that enable them to contribute while being true to themselves.

Mature people who aspire to be winners seek environments that foster creativity, encourage responsible risk taking, and enable them to grow and develop. Variety, tailoring and the tolerance of very different approaches is often the key to corporate success and individual fulfilment.

Building a community of people who are open minded and free thinking may be a more sensible strategy than the adoption of a complete framework such as quality that may end up acting as a protective cocoon. Many people throughout the ages would not have been innovators if they had been equipped with a standard tool-kit that caused them to look at the world and its problems in the same way as everyone else. They had the courage to attract or create whatever capability and competencies were relevant to the opportunities they defined and the markets their imaginations created.

In conclusion, the emphasis should be upon values and relationships roles, competencies and behaviours rather then procedures and structures; flexibility and intuition rather than prescriptive and mechanical approaches, the fostering of diversity and creativity rather than the enforcement of standards; learning rather than control. Management also needs to be holistic to understand interrelationships between elements and assemble the combination of them that will deliver multiple objectives and longer-term goals such as renewal and transformation. People should be beneficiaries of change and not its victims.

The options, examples and opportunities examined in the course of preparing 'The Future of the Organization' suggest that, given a shared sense of purpose, supportive learning partners, and an appropriate mix of change elements, renewal and transformation can be achieved. The potential payoffs – both for ourselves and for others – more than justify the incremental effort involved.

Further Information

* 'The Future of the Organisation: Achieving Excellence through Business Transformation' (1997/8) by Colin Coulson-Thomas is published by Kogan Page.

CHAPTER 27

CREATING A COMPANY THAT CAN COMPETE AND WIN

In many sectors different companies appear to have similar competitive strategies. As was mentioned in chapter 1, they recruit from the same business schools, buy the same technologies and employ standard processes. Yet some expand and prosper while others decline. Despite a decade of re-engineering, a succession of management fads, heavy investment in IT and extensive use of management consultants, many companies struggle to cope. What do the businesses that adapt and grow do differently?

Most if not all of the surveys carried out within the winning companies, winning people research programme have been concerned with improving competitiveness, including those carried out to identify critical success factors in particular areas. Over 1,400 companies have participated in this group of studies. Projects have been undertaken to increase the competitiveness of over 150 companies, and over 400 organisations are known to have used methodologies and approaches developed within the programme to improve their competitiveness.

We return to this central question which for more than a decade has inspired a research programme led by the author (see Introduction, page xv), which has examined why some companies win new business, build customer relationships, create and exploit know-how and manage change while others stagnate. Research teams compare the approaches and practices of the most and least successful, and isolate critical success factors for competing and winning*. This chapter attempts a summary of what we have learned.

The collective experience of over 2,000 enterprises across many sectors reveals how profitable and expanding companies – the winners – become and remain competitive. People in these businesses don't print money or cheat. Their attitudes, approaches, perspectives and priorities ensure they win the battle to change, re-invent and break free of past constraints.

If you and your colleagues are frustrated and would like to transform the fortunes of your company you can indeed learn from those who succeed. The key lessons – and stark differences between winners and losers – can be expressed in terms of 'do's' and 'don'ts'.

Let's start with what you are setting out to achieve. Survival – getting through the next quarter or twelve months – does not energize and excite. Be positive. Craft and communicate a distinctive vision, a compelling purpose, stretching goals and clear objectives.

Remain relevant and stay vital. Develop additional income streams, enhance capabilities and refresh intellectual capital. Create additional options and extend choice. Launch new ventures and establish new markets.

Display the will to win. Winners are driven to succeed. Their actions demonstrate they care. Read the road ahead. Anticipate events and confront realities. Take a longer-term view and provide strategic leadership. Ensure immediate priorities do not take precedence over longer-term aims.

Inspire and motivate. Lead and guide. Make sure people understand what they need to do, are visibly committed, and are prepared, equipped and enabled to act. Identify and tackle barriers to change. Don't sidetrack critics, conceal disappointments or rationalize failure.

However keen you are to go forward, don't make changes for change's sake. Change can be stressful and it may disrupt valued relationships. Think before you act. Assess likely consequences. Balance change and continuity. Distinguish goals, values, objectives, policies and activities that need to be changed from those that should be continued.

Don't expend energy in peripheral areas or bark up the wrong trees. Concentrate your effort where it is most likely to make a difference. Focus upon the critical success factors for achieving key corporate objectives and delivering greater customer and shareholder value.

Understand your customers. Ensure they are not disadvantaged by change. Put yourself out to develop tailored responses. Deliver bespoke offerings to them. Be proactive. Don't wait to be asked. Take the initiative. Identify and approach those you would like to do business with. Push back the boundaries of what is possible, and aim to become a sought-after and trusted business partner.

Don't adopt standard approaches or be rigid and inflexible. Think for yourself rather than imitate and copy others. Jumping upon bandwaggons and 'me-too' activities are not the route to market leadership. Don't be overly cautious and too wary of commitments. Don't respond belatedly to events or fail to anticipate requirements and implications.

Be confident. Don't be indecisive or oblivious to the needs of others. Build and release talent. Explore, pioneer and discover. Encourage and support enterprise and innovation.

Losers are complacent, secretive and defensive. Don't keep things to yourself or be reluctant to delegate. Trust other people and share information and opportunities with them where this is likely to prove mutually beneficial. Empathise and invite feedback. Question and challenge, and listen and learn.

Build relationships, but select people, business partners and opportunities with care. Don't end up playing other people's games. At the same time, don't focus exclusively upon your own agenda. Collaborate on the basis of openness and transparency with complementary spirits who share your vision and values.

Be persistent but pragmatic, and determined but adaptable in pursuit of your aims. Take calculated risks. Experiment with new ways of working, learning and collaborating.

The board should help you to compete and win. It should be the heart and soul of a company, the source of its ambition and drive. Without a sense of purpose, a sound strategy and the will to achieve, well-endowed corporations wither and die. Whether or not a company achieves and sustains success depends largely upon the attitudes and conduct of its directors.

Don't mouth generalizations, engage in spin or confuse activity with progress. Cut through blather and hype. Get down to the fundamentals of what needs to be done. Wherever possible, adopt simple solutions and take direct action. Regard change, renewal and transformation as normal activities.

Don't try to do everything yourself or resist new and external ideas. Work with colleagues to foster winning attitudes and behaviours. Balance strategy with capability and think holistically. Ensure all the pieces of the jigsaw puzzle required for successful transformation and sustained competitiveness are in place.

Directors and senior managers cannot become directly involved in the many and varied activities needed to respond imaginatively to changing circumstances. Empower business units and venture teams to bring about whatever changes are required to enable them to achieve their objectives and deliver value to *their* customers.

New areas of risk can arise as structures, processes and systems are reviewed and altered. Make sure people understand what is at stake and are ready to respond. Problems will arise. Their absence could indicate a lack of ambition. Learning from them and celebrating success help to sustain momentum.

Finally – as has been stressed before – go for it. The prospects of 'loser' companies can be transformed by putting the critical success factors required for winning in place. Achieving success is often easier and is invariably more satisfying than rationalising failure.

Further Information

* Details of various reports covering critical success factors in particular areas that are vital for competing and winning – including those listed in Appendix A can be obtained from Policy Publications.

CHAPTER 28

ACHIEVE COMMERCIAL SUCCESS AND PERSONAL FULFILMENT

ENTREPRENEURSHIP FOR BOTH INDIVIDUALS AND THE ENTERPRISE

Earlier chapters of this book have focused upon different aspects of securing profitable corporate growth and business development. This final chapter argues it is possible to make money and be true to oneself, i.e. one can achieve both commercial success and personal fulfilment.

The experience of the 215 companies surveyed in relation to bringing about change suggests the prospects of successful implementation are significantly improved if what is being proposed benefits the people involved as well as their employing organisations. Similarly a pan-European investigation of new ways of working involving over 100 organisations found that participation and creating benefits for the people concerned speeded up the delivery of projects. Work undertaken to build support tools has consciously included ways of making it much easier for those affected to do their jobs.

Many people are creating profitable businesses while doing what they enjoy doing and do best. Individuals and organisations can both benefit if they understand personal aspirations and respond appropriately.

From time to time many individuals consider a change of direction. Some seek a more equitable balance between work and life, or want more control over their destiny. Others harbour a desire to become entrepreneurs. They are fed up being a piece on someone else's chess board and want to play their own game.

People can experience a range of emotions from apprehension on starting work to a mid-life crisis. They question what they are doing with their lives. Sometimes imagined or available alternatives seem to bring their own problems and uncertainties. People weigh the advantages and disadvantages of different courses of action. They assess whether the risks and costs involved will outweigh desired benefits. They wonder whether the grass really will be greener on the other side of the fence.

Certain business trends have implications for both individuals and employers. For example, as more customers demand bespoke responses, front line staff dealing with them increasingly need to think and act like entrepreneurs. This opens up an historic window of opportunity to reconcile people and organisations.

An investigation into emerging opportunities for entrepreneurship has examined how people can best respond. The findings – along with self-assessment exercises and checklists – are set out in 'Individuals and Enterprise', a guide for intending entrepreneurs*. They reveal the satisfaction and excitement people can derive from discovering their inner selves, breaking free and changing course.

Most people have opportunities to be true to their ideals and beliefs. Most could either start a new enterprise or make fundamental changes in their current organisation. Challenges such as career uncertainty, new forms of working and even redundancy can be turned into exciting opportunities for going it alone or collaborating with an existing employer to create a new offering or launch a new venture.

Let's look as what those who succeed financially while also being personally fulfilled do differently. Firstly, they acknowledge that all is not well with their existing lives. Whether or not they experience demons in the night they recognise what is missing. They assess their current situation and decide that enough is enough.

Life's winners also recognise the dawn of a new era of opportunity. They both search for and recognise what is latent and hidden. They are alert to trends such as falling barriers. They view emerging concerns, current problems and likely changes as potential sources of opportunity. They consider how such developments will affect them and others, and assess what new qualities, careers, lifestyle options, strategies, offerings and markets will be required to cope with them and benefit from them.

Next, our winners look at what it would take to succeed in the new arenas of opportunity they identify. They consider changing requirements, the limitations of current approaches and potential conflicts of interest. They assess themselves and review their current circumstances and obligations in relation to the essence of what will be required for an effective response.

The most fulfilled devote more time to the question: who am I? They are much more self-aware. They seek to understand the person within and assess which opportunities – if pursued – would most allow them to be true to their inner selves. Organisations too need to assess themselves in relation to new requirements and opportunities, and consider the implications for ways of working and future relationships with people whose aspirations may be changing.

Smart intending entrepreneurs consider opportunities for collaboration before they burn their boats, leave their employer and launch out on their own. They explore options for cooperation, buy-out possibilities and the scope for working with rather than for organisations. Confident companies do likewise. They consider whether they should become a sponsor or business partner rather than an employer, and encourage aspiring entrepreneurs to become internal intrapreneurs or joint venture colleagues.

Successful entrepreneurs look at the world differently and retain a sense of wonder and excitement at the possibilities. They question, probe and explore. They bring new combinations of elements together and assemble winning formulae. When the time is right they seize the moment and have a go.

Winners recognise leeches and parasites, but they also appreciate collective endeavour and understand the value of the right networks and relationships. If appropriate, they operate in collaboration with others. They are not afraid to ask for help, but select colleagues with care. They seek soul mates who share their visions. They attract contributors, energetic business builders with complementary qualities.

Rather than imitate and copy others the most fulfilled 'do it their way'. They recognise individuality, both in themselves and in others. They achieve a healthy balance between reflection and action, and secure flexible access to the capabilities they need to turn their dreams into a reality. They avoid siren voices and the vanity of size, seeking a scale of operation that is right for the opportunities they pursue.

Confident leaders view the entrepreneurial aspirations of their people as an opportunity rather than a threat. They call for proposals and back the most promising ones. They provide corporate support services to help intending entrepreneurs get started. In return for a share of new ventures they offer finance, development advice and access to a customer base.

Further information

*'Individuals and Enterprise: creating entrepreneurs for the new millennium through personal transformation' (1999) and 'Shaping Things to Come, strategies for creating alternative enterprises' (2001) – a guide for creating new offerings – are published by Blackhall Publishing.

APPENDIX A

'WINNING BUSINESS' RESEARCH AND BEST PRACTICE PROGRAMME

PROJECT LEADER: PROF. COLIN COULSON-THOMAS

The 'winning business' best practice programme is identifying the critical success factors for winning and retaining customers in competitive markets. Over 2,000 companies and professional practices have participated. The business practices of 'winners' are being compared with those of 'losers' to reveal why some companies are so much more successful than others. The investigating teams are led by Prof. Colin Coulson-Thomas of the University of Lincoln, an experienced chairman of entrepreneurial and award winning companies, and chairman of the judges for the e-Business Innovations Awards.

Recent outputs include 'critical success factors' reports, 'best practice' case studies, practical bidding tools and techniques, key business development skills, in-house training and a benchmarking service which provides companies with bespoke reports highlighting where they most lag behind successful competitors. Published best practice reports that are currently available include:

- '*Winning New Business: the Critical Success Factors*' which examines the processes and practices for winning business in competitive situations of over 300 companies.
- '*Bidding for Business in Construction, IT & Telecoms, Engineering and Manufacturing, etc.*,' best practice resource packs which include

reports on critical success factors for winning business in particular sectors.

- '*Bidding for Business: the Skills Agenda*' which covers the top 20 skills required.
- '*The Contract Bid Manager's Toolkit*' containing 30 practical tools for winning contracts.
- '*Winning New Business in Management Consultancy, Advertising, Accountancy, PR & Marketing Consultancy, Engineering Consultancy, IT Consultancy, Law*, etc., *the Critical Success Factors*' covering particular professions.
- '*Developing Strategic Customers & Key Accounts: the Critical Success Factors*' examines the experiences and key customer relationship practices of 194 companies.
- The '*Close to the Customer*' series of 28 management briefings on particular customer relationship management issues and best practice in different business sectors.
- '*Developing a Corporate Learning Strategy*' which examines training and development practices and priorities, and information and knowledge entrepreneurship.
- '*Effective Purchasing: the Critical Success Factors*', a European study of issues & trends.
- '*Managing Intellectual Capital to Grow Shareholder Value*' an examination of how the better management of intellectual capital might generate incremental income.
- '*Pricing for Profit*' which shows how 'leader' companies achieve the benefits of effective pricing.

All of these reports and the 'Close to the Customer' series of briefings on customer relationship management are published by Policy Publications Ltd. Further information: www.ntwkfirm.com/policy-publications.

APPENDIX B

FURTHER READING

SELECTED PUBLICATIONS ON LEADING PERFORMANCE IMPROVEMENT AND CORPORATE TRANSFORMATION

This Appendix lists some of the publications by Colin Coulson-Thomas that have been produced to disseminate the results of the research programme undertaken by Prof. Colin Coulson-Thomas (CCT) and described in the Introduction (page xv) and Appendix A.

Selected Core Publications

Books

'Transforming the Company, Bridging the Gap Between Management Myth & Corporate Reality', London, Kogan Page 1992 and also (see below) 'Transforming the Company, Manage Change, Compete and Win', London, Kogan Page 2002 and 2004 (paperback).

[The first edition summarises and integrates a decade of research by Prof. Colin Coulson-Thomas PhD (CCT) up to 1991 and provided the agenda for subsequent research by CCT during the decade 1992–2001 (summarised in the second edition published in 2002 – see below) that examined why some directors and boards are more successful than others at leading performance improvement and corporate transformation and closing certain key gaps between aspiration and achievement. It synthesises findings from 15 (37 second edition, see below) published research reports authored or co-authored by CCT that relate to the achievement of corporate transformation to a more flexible and responsive model of operation. These surveys and related research undertaken for the book revealed the extent to which management practice and directorial rhetoric differed from management theory and corporate reality. This book was among the first on re-engineering to champion more holistic and people-centred approaches to transformation.]

'Creating Excellence in the Boardroom', London, McGraw-Hill (in the Henley Management series), 1993 (currently being updated with recent findings)

'Developing Directors: Building an Effective Boardroom Team', London, McGraw-Hill, 1993 (currently being updated with recent findings)

[These two related books are concerned with direction, understanding and improving board performance and the role and effectiveness of the board in relation to leading performance improvement and corporate transformation and business development.]

[Editor and contributor of three chapters] 'Business Process Re-engineering: Myth & Reality', London, Kogan Page, 1994 and [paperback edition] September 1996, 254pp

[Core chapters by CCT summarised the COBRA approach and methodology which constitutes a distinctly European approach to re-engineering and corporate transformation. One of the books by CCT that has been translated: [editor and contributor] Reengenharia Dos Processos Empresariais: mito & realidade Rio de Janeiro and Sao Paulo, Brasil, Editoria Record, 1996].]

The Future of the Organisation: Achieving Excellence through Business Transformation, London, Kogan Page, 1997 and [paperback edition] 1998.

[Incorporates further research findings relating to the use of improvement, change and transformation approaches, methodologies and tools and updates those advocated in 'Transforming the Company' in the light of experience with certain suites of methodologies CCT has edited (e.g. for strategic use of IT).]

Transforming the Company, Manage Change, Compete and Win, London, Kogan Page, 2002 and paperback edition 2004

[Summarises and integrates a further decade of research by CCT. An updated and substantially re-written second edition of 'Transforming the Company' (1992, see above) to incorporate 'critical success factor' findings and 'winner/leader' and 'loser/laggard' comparisons relating to major routes and challenges to the achievement of performance improvement and corporate transformation from 22 published research reports based upon surveys and investigations undertaken or led by CCT during the period 1992–2001. This research specifically addressed the more significant and under-researched issues identified by the pre-1992 research either undertaken for or summarised in the first edition.]

Research Reports

The 15 research reports based on research undertaken by CCT and upon which the first edition of 'Transforming the Company' (1992) draws include some that have led to subsequent developments. For example:

'The Responsive Organisation, People Management, the Challenge of the 1990s', (Joint with Richard Brown), London, British Institute of Management, 1989
'The Flat Organisation: Philosophy and Practice' (Joint with Trudy Coe) Corby, British Institute of Management, 1991
'Professional Development of and for the Board', London, Institute of Directors, January 1990

The Role and Status of Project Management, London, An Adaptation Ltd survey for the Association of Project Managers (APM), 1990

Selected findings from this survey are summarised in: Project Management, a necessary skill? Industrial Management & Data Systems, No. 6, 1990, pp 17–21

[Study of the leadership and management of re-engineering and corporate transformation projects resulted in this further research.]

'Beyond Quality: Managing the Relationship with the Customer', (joint with Richard Brown), Corby, British Institute of Management, 1990

'Quality the Next Steps' (Joint with Susan D Coulson-Thomas), London, Adaptation Ltd, 1991

(Principal Author and Editor) 'Business Restructuring and Teleworking', Brussels, European Commission, 1994

[The main initial report produced by the EU COBRA project which represented a systematic pan-European investigation of business restructuring, re-engineering and new ways of working across Europe.]

Methodology

(Principal Author/Executive Editor): 'The Responsive Organisation' (3 volume boxed set of reports), Bedford, Policy Publications, 1995

[A detailed version of the six-stage COBRA methodology for introducing new ways of working (eg. teleworking) while re-engineering to improve/ transform performance, together with 21 illustrative case studies and reviews of 101 tools and techniques referred to within the COBRA methodology. Other published versions of the COBRA methodology include one for re-engineering supply chains using e-commerce technologies (The Competitive Network, 1996).

[Summary descriptions of aspects and/or versions of the 'teleworking' version of the COBRA methodology appear in various sets of conference proceedings. For example:

> Corporate Re-structuring and Telework, in Telework Congress: Chance and Challenge for Europe, Luxembourg, 26 to 28 June 1996, Luxembourg, Office for Official Publications of the European Communities, 1996 pp 174–217

[Several subsequent research reports by CCT contain process checklists, models and/or suggested processes for the review and improvement of particular categories of process. These and other related methodologies developed by CCT (e.g. a detailed methodology for reviewing and improving processes and practices for winning business) incorporate critical success factors identified by related research reports.]

Articles

Certain articles by Colin Coulson-Thomas also disseminate the findings of published research reports by CCT from which 'Transforming the Company' (1992) and/or more recent books by CCT have drawn and integrated relevant findings, including:

- Developing Directors, European Management Journal, Vol. 8 No 4, December 1990, pp 488–499
- Competent Directors: Boardroom Myths and Realities Journal of General Management, Vol. 17 No. 1 Autumn 1991, pp 1–26
- The Responsive Organisation, Journal of General Management, Vol. 15, No 4 Summer 1990, pp 21–31
- Customers Marketing and the Network Organisation, Journal of Marketing Management, 1991, Vol. 7, pp 237–255
- IT Directors and IT Strategy, Journal of Information Technology, 1991, 6, pp 192–203
- Directors and IT, and IT Directors, European Journal of Information Systems, Volume 1, No 1, 1991, pp 45–53
- Quality: Where do we go from here? International Journal of Quality & Reliability Management, Volume 9 No I, 1992, pp38–55.
- Strategic Vision or Strategic Con?: Rhetoric or Reality, Long Range Planning, Volume 25, No 1, 1992, pp81–89
- Developing Competent Directors and Effective Boards, Journal of Management Development, Vol. 11, No. 1, 1992, pp 39–49
- Developing Directors: Building an Effective Boardroom Team, Journal of European Industrial Training, Vol. 18, No. 6, 1994, pp 29–52
- (with Stephen Drew) Transformation through teamwork: the path to the new organisation? Management Decision, Vol. 34, No. 1, 1996 pp 7–17
- Business Process Re-engineering and Strategic Change, Strategic Change, Vol. 5 No. 3, May–June 1996, pp 165–178
- Business Process Re-engineering and Teleworking, Business Process Re-engineering & Management Journal, Vol. 1 No 2, 1995, pp 47–57
- Creating an Effective Board, Round Table on Company Boards and Directors, IIMB Management Review [Journal of the Indian Institute of Management, Bangalore], Vol. 9. No. 1, January–March 1997, pp 37–47

- Business Transformation: Relevance and Risks, IIMB Management Review [Journal of the Indian Institute of Management, Bangalore], Vol. 9, No. 4, October–December 1997, pp 37–48
- Managing innovation in public services: European and international experience, Total Quality Management, Vol. 9, Nos 2 & 3, 1998 pp 213–222
- The relative roles and risks of change and continuity, Strategic Change, Vol. 7 No. 8, December 1998, pp 449–458
- Managing the Virtual Corporation, IIMB Management Review [Journal of the Indian Institute of Management, Bangalore], Vol. 10 No. 3, July–September 1998, pp 5–14
- Developing a corporate learning strategy: creating intrapreneurs, Strategic Change, Volume 9 Number 8, December 2000, pp 469–479

Selected Related Publications

Books

'Creating the Global Company: Successful Internationalisation', London, McGraw-Hill (in the Henley Management series), 1992

[Articles on key findings include:

> Internationalisation and the Global Company European Business Review, Vol. 93, No. 2, 1993, pp42–44]

Individuals and Enterprise, Creating Entrepreneurs for the New Millennium Through Personal Transformation, Dublin, Blackhall Publishing, 1999
Shaping Things to Come, strategies for creating alternative enterprises, Dublin, Blackhall Publishing, 2001

[Two books written for (intending) entrepreneurs drawing upon the findings of ABUITTS and other research projects, with exercises to improve/transform entrepreneurial performance and stimulate more imaginative approaches to the business development process.]

The Information Entrepreneur, changing requirements for corporate and individual success, Winnersh, 3Com Active Business Unit, 2000

'The Knowledge Entrepreneur' (with accompanying CD-ROM disc on the use of support tools incorporating identified critical success factors), London, Kogan Page, 2003

[Two books based upon research projects undertaken by CCT to understand and improve the end-to-end process of knowledge creation, management and exploitation. The Knowledge Entrepreneur draws upon recent development projects to incorporate into knowledge-based support tools critical success factors identified by 17 of the published research reports.]

Chapters

Contributions to The Financial Times Handbook of Management (1995):

- Re-engineering in Practise, The Financial Times Handbook of Management. Edited by Stuart Crainer, FT/Pitman, London 1995, pp 245–256
- Creating an Effective Board, The Financial Times Handbook of Management. Edited by Stuart Crainer, FT/Pitman, London 1995, pp 1070–1080

Corporate Culture in Norman A Hart (Editor), Strategic Public Relations, London, Macmillan, 1995, pp 248–275

Research Reports

Other research reports contributing findings to 'Transforming the Company' (1992) include:

'The New Professionals' British Institute of Management: London (1988)

[Related articles include:

Higher and Further Education and the Professions The International Journal of Educational Management, volume 3, No. 3, 1989, pp 4–6]

Communicating for Change, (Joint with Susan Coulson-Thomas), London, an Adaptation Ltd survey for Granada Business Services, 1991

'Human Resource Development for International Operation', a Survey sponsored by Surrey European Management School, Adaptation Ltd., London (1990)

'The Effective Board, Current Practice, Myths and Realities', a discussion document, (Joint with Alan Wakelam) Institute of Directors (1991)

'Induction Package for New TEC Directors', TEC Secretariat, Redditch (1993)

[A multi-media package to improve board performance based upon research undertaken by CCT, and subsequently widely used within the TEC movement.]

'Harnessing the Potential of Groups', London, Adaptation Ltd., London (1993)

[Subsequent research on bid team performance led to the first of 18 research reports on the winning business process, which also drew upon experience of using the COBRA approach.]

Developing a Corporate Learning Strategy, the key knowledge management challenge for the HR function, Bedford, Policy Publications, 1999

[An examination of the knowledge creation sub-process, the performance of corporate training and development policies, and the knowledge created by their activities.]

Since 1995 CCT has led 18 research projects to examine critical success factors and performance improvement/transformation opportunities in relation to particular aspects of winning business, or processes and practices for winning business in particular sectors and seven professions. The two most recent research reports are:

- Pricing for Profit, the critical success factors, Bedford, Policy Publications (in association with the Chartered Institute of Marketing), 2002

- (Joint), Winning New Business, the critical success factors (with an accompanying CD-ROM disc on the use of support tools incorporating identified critical success factors), Bedford, Policy Publications, 2003

Methodologies

Various versions of the methodologies developed by EU projects to adapt the COBRA approach have appeared in country specific versions. For example, in relation to ABUITTS:

- [Principal Author] COBRA: A Methodology for the SME Environment, ABUITSS Seminar Background Material, Part B, Guecho, CARSA, 1966, 66 pages
- [Principal Author] COBRA: A Methodology for the SME Environment, ABUITSS Seminar Background Material Part B [Greek Translation], Athens, EUROCOM, July 1996, 94 pages

Articles have also been used to disseminate such methodologies for improving or transforming performance. For example, in relation to HOCAPRIT:

- Re-engineering Hospital and Health Care Processes, British Journal of Healthcare Management, Vol. 2, No 6, 1996, pp 338–342
- Process management in a hospital and healthcare context: Evidence of the HOCAPRIT project, Business Process Management Journal, Vol. 3, No. 2, 1997, pp 118–132.

Articles

Selected articles by Colin Coulson-Thomas relating to improving and/or transforming performance through new ways of working and alternative models of operation:

- Homeworking and the Rank Xerox Networking Programme International Journal of Technology Management, Vol. 4, No. 1, 1989, pp 95–101

- Information Technology and the Responsive Organisation, Information Technology & Public Policy, Vol. 8, No. 1, Winter 1989, pp 29–30
- Responsive Professional and Educational Organisations, International Journal of Manpower, Vol. 10, No. 6, 1989, pp 13–16
- Creating the Responsive Organisation: Implementing Teleworking, Understanding Workplace Flexibility, Vol. 8 No. 2, December 1998, 14pp
- Encouraging partnering and collaboration, Industrial and Commercial Training, Vol. 37 No. 4, 2005, pp 179–184

Selected articles by Colin Coulson-Thomas on board performance and people aspects of corporate transformation:

- Human Resource: The critical success factor The Leadership & Organisation Development Journal, Vol. 10, No. 4, 1989, pp 13–16
- Career Paths to the Boardroom, The International Journal of Career Management, vol. 2, No. 3, 1990, pp 26–32
- Developing Tomorrow's Professionals Today Journal of European Industrial Training, Vol. 15, No. 1, 1991, pp 3–11
- What the Personnel Director Can Bring to the Boardroom Table Personnel Management, October 1991, pp 36–39
- Developing Directors/Vdvikling af bestyrelses-medlemmer, LEDELSE I DAG No 4, Autumn 1991, pp 16–26
- Directorial Competence, Analysis, Competency, Vol. 1, No. 4, Summer 1994, pp 18–20
- Harnessing the Board's Potential, Corporate Governance: An International Review, Vol. 2, No. 3, July 1994, pp 135–137
- Competencies for business process re-engineering, Competency, Vol. 2, No. 1, Autumn 1994, pp 35–39
- The future of the organization: selected management and development issues, Industrial and Commercial Training, Vol. 29, No. 7, 1997, pp 204–207
- Competency and the future of the organisation, Competency, Vol. 5, No. 1, Autumn 1997, pp 21–26
- Careers, development and the future of the organisation, Career Development International, Vol. 3, No. 1, 1998, pp 13–17

- Who dares wins, People Management, Vol. 5 No. 17, 2 September 1999, pp 44–49 [Wie waagt, die wint, Human Resource Management select, Jaargang 12, No. 1, 2000, pp 78–85]
- Creating a winning board: differing approaches of the boards of successful and struggling companies, Industrial and Commercial Training, Vol. 37, No. 2, 2005, pp 67–72
- Corporate governance: develop questioning directors and a winning board, Developing HR Strategy, Issue 3, July 2005, pp 22–25

Selected articles by Colin Coulson-Thomas relating to IT aspects of performance improvement and/or transformation:

- Breaking Through the Information Barrier: Management Development and IT International Journal of Technology Management, Volume 5, No. 5, 1990, pp 618–623
- Breaking Through the Information Barrier: Management Development and IT International Journal of Computer Applications in Technology, Volume 3, No. 4, 1990, pp 269–271 [see also: Education & Training, Volume 32, No. 1, 1990, pp 10–13]
- IT and New Forms of Organisation for Knowledge Workers: Opportunity and implementation, Employee Relations, Vol. 13, No. 4, 1991, pp 22–32
- Management en IT, IT Management, Management en organisatie van automatiseringsmiddelen, 1992, 4, pp 115–130
- Using job support tools to increase workgroup performance, International Journal of Productivity and Performance Management, Vol. 54, No. 3, 2005, pp 206–211

Selected articles by Colin Coulson-Thomas on business process re-engineering and corporate transformation:

- Corporate Transformation and Business Process Re-engineering Executive Development, Vol. 6, No. 1, 1993, pp 14–20
- Tough Love: COBRA Project, International Corporate Re-engineering, Vol. 2, Issue 2, pp 18–22

- Business Restructuring Across Europe: Business Process Re-engineering and Teleworking, Business Change & Re-engineering, Vol. 2 No 3, 1995 pp 51–60
- Business Process Re-engineering: the Development Requirements and Implications, Executive Development, Vol. 8, No 2, 1995, pp 3–6
- Business Process Re-engineering: The Boardroom Implications, Research Report, Corporate Governance, An International Review, Vol. 3, No 4, October 1995, pp 235–240
- BPR and the learning organisation, The Learning Organisation Vol. 3, No. 1, 1996, pp 16–21
- Business process re-engineering and teleworking, Industrial and Commercial Training, Vol. 28 No. 1, 1996, pp 12–15
- The Future of the Organization: The Case for More Holistic Approaches, The International Journal of Business Transformation, Vol. 1 No. 2, October 1997, pp 117–126
- Europe's Problems with Re-engineering, European Quality, Vol. 4 No. 1, 1997, pp 34–37; [Trans. By P. van der Karl] Europe's Problems with Reengineering [original article in European Quality, Vol. 4 No. 1, 1997], Human Resource Management-select, No. 3, 1997, pp 80–87

Selected articles by Colin Coulson-Thomas on transforming business and enterprise development processes:

- Winning Major Contracts: Could Your Company's Performance be Improved? The Internat. Journal of Business Transformation, Vol. 1 No. 4, April 1998, pp 258–260
- Individuals and enterprise: developing intrapreneurs for the new millennium, Industrial and Commercial Training, Vol. 31, No. 7, 1999, pp 258–261
- Individuals and enterprise: creating e-business intrapreneurs and corporate ventures, Competency & Emotional Intelligence, Vol. 7, No. 3, Spring 2000, pp. 42–44
- Individuals and enterprise: winning business in the new millennium, Industrial and Commercial Training, Vol. 32, No. 1, 2000, pp. 4–8
- Shaping things to come, strategies for creating alternative enterprises, Industrial and Commercial Training, Vol. 33, No. 5, 2001, pp 154–156

- Shaping things to come, strategies for creating alternative enterprises, Competency & Emotional Intelligence, Vol. 8, No. 4, Summer 2001, pp 30–32
- Developing and supporting information entrepreneurs, Career Development International, Vol. 6, No. 4, 2001, pp 231–235
- Shaping things to come, strategies for creating alternative enterprises, Scenario and strategy planning, Vol. 3, Issue 2, June/July 2001, pp 12–14
- Entrepreneurship for organisational success, Journal of Professional HRM, Innovation and Entrepreneurship, Issue No. 22, January 2001, pp 25–31

Selected articles by Colin Coulson-Thomas on the relative success of differing approaches to directing and leading performance improvement and corporate transformation:

- Why do some succeed in managing change while others fail? How to handle ... Change management, Accounting & Business, June 2002, pp 36–37
- A matter of conduct, Chartered Secretary, October 2002, pp 27–29
- Applied Corporate Governance, A Matter of Conduct, Keeping Good Companies, Vol. 54 No. 11, December 2002, pp 658–660
- A Sound Board, Quality World, Vol. 29 Issue 1, January 2003, pp 20–23
- Transforming the company: the differing learning practices of successful and unsuccessful companies, Industrial and Commercial Training, Vol. 35 No. 1, 2003, pp 5–10
- Successful and unsuccessful approaches to working with consultants, Keeping good companies, Vol. 57 No. 1, February 2005, pp 51–53
- Creating a Competitive Company, Developing HR Strategy, Issue 1, March 2005, pp 14–16

Selected articles by Colin Coulson-Thomas on improving learning processes and new approaches to learning:

- Campus or Learning Network? Is IT the problem or a solution? Information Technology & Learning, Volume 12, No. 3, February 1990, pp 91–93

- Building Europe's Learning Foundations, The European Learning Network, IT in Europe Journal, February 1990, pp 14–19
- Integrating Learning and Working, Industrial and Commercial Training, Vol. 24, No. 10, 1992, pp 18–22
- Using management methodologies, tools and techniques: the need to value behaviours, feelings and values, Competency & Emotional Intelligence, Vol. 12, No.2, Winter (2004/05), pp 38–40

Selected articles by Colin Coulson-Thomas on improving knowledge creation, management and exploitation processes:

- The Future of the Organization: Selected Knowledge Management Issues, The Journal of Knowledge Management, Vol. 1, No. 1, September 1997, pp 15–26
- Developing a corporate learning strategy, Industrial and Commercial Training, Vol. 32, No. 3, 2000, pp. 84–88
- Building learning competencies and capabilities, Competency & Emotional Intelligence Quarterly, 2000, Vol. 7, No. 2, Winter 1999/00, pp. 31–33
- Developing and supporting information entrepreneurs, Industrial and Commercial Training, Volume 32, Number 6, 2000 pp 196–200
- Managing Knowledge and Intellectual Capital to Grow Shareholder Value, Company Secretary's Factbook, March 2001, pp 1–15
- Opportunity Knocks, Knowledge Management, Volume 4, Issue 5, February 2001, pp 31–34
- Developing a Corporate Learning Strategy, Int. Journal of Information Technology and Management, Vol. 2, Nos 1/2, 2003, pp 151–156
- Managing Intellectual Capital to Grow Shareholder Value, Int. Journal of Information Technology and Management, Vol. 2, Nos 1/2, 2003, pp 157–161

CCT has also authored over 50 further articles on performance improvement and corporate transformation in journals aimed at particular communities of practitioners, eg. those aimed at quality practitioners include:

- Managing Culture Change, Managing Service Quality, Vol. 1, No. 4, May 1991, pp 187–192
- Responsible Customer Management, The TQM Magazine, Vol. 3, No. 2, April 1991, pp 81–86
- Surveying the Scene, The TQM Magazine, Volume 4, No 1, February 1992, pp 25–31
- The Virtual Challenge, European Quality, Vol. 4, No. 6, December 1997, pp 48–51
- The future of the organisation: the role and contribution of quality, Managing Service Quality, Vol. 7, No. 6, 1997, pp 301–306
- Tailor Made, Quality World, Vol. 29, Issue 6, June 2003, pp 32–35

[Articles by CCT on successive research outputs have been placed in certain journals on a regular basis to reach groups such as: communicators (eg. Internal Communications); internal management specialists (eg. Management Services); and external consultants (eg. Management Consultancy, Professional Consulting) who are either directly involved in performance improvement and corporate transformation activities, or are in a position to influence them, such as accountants (eg. accounting and business) and company secretaries (eg. the ICSA journal).]

APPENDIX C

MASTERCLASSES AND WORKSHOPS

DESIGN YOUR OWN MASTERCLASS, SEMINAR OR WORKSHOP

Prof. Colin Coulson-Thomas has presentations, exercises and handouts on the topics listed below.

Assemble a combination of the modules below to address your particular development needs.

Each module is based upon key findings from one or more of Prof. Colin Coulson-Thomas's recent books or reports and benefits from his continuing work with ambitious boards, management teams and entrepreneurs.

Introduction (Setting the Scene)

- Learning from best practice
- Critical success factors for competing and winning
- The strategic opportunity
- The key contribution of the board and senior management team

Colin Coulson-Thomas, 'Transforming the Company, manage change, compete and win' (Kogan Page, 2002 & 2004), chapters 1 and 2

Understanding the Business Environment

- Issue monitoring and management

Colin Coulson-Thomas, 'Transforming the Company, manage change, compete and win' (Kogan Page, 2002 & 2004), chapter 10

Colin Coulson-Thomas, 'Shaping Things to Come, strategies for creating alternative enterprises' (Blackhall Publishing, 2001)

Understanding the company's marketplace

- Changing aspirations of customers/employees
- Matching individual and corporate aspirations

Colin Coulson-Thomas, 'Transforming the Company, manage change, compete and win' (Kogan Page, 2002 & 2004), chapter 10

Colin Coulson-Thomas, 'Individuals and Enterprise, creating entrepreneurs for the new millennium through personal transformation' (Blackhall Publishing, 1999)

Visioning

- Establishing stakeholder requirements
- Establishing a corporate vision, goals and strategic objectives
- Assessing the gap between aspiration and achievement

Colin Coulson-Thomas, 'Transforming the Company, manage change, compete and win' (Kogan Page, 2002 & 2004), chapter 4

Leadership

- Providing Strategic Leadership
- Leading effective teams

Colin Coulson-Thomas, 'Transforming the Company, manage change, compete and win' (Kogan Page, 2002 & 2004), chapter 3

Colin Coulson-Thomas, 'Creating Excellence in the Boardroom, A guide to shaping directorial competence and board effectiveness' (McGraw-Hill, 1993)

Colin Coulson-Thomas, 'Developing Directors, building an effective boardroom team' (McGraw-Hill, 1993)

Creating an effective board

- Good Corporate Governance
- Selecting and Developing Directors

Colin Coulson-Thomas, 'Transforming the Company, manage change, compete and win' (Kogan Page, 2002 & 2004), chapter 3

Colin Coulson-Thomas, 'Creating Excellence in the Boardroom, A guide to shaping directorial competence and board effectiveness' (McGraw-Hill, 1993)

Colin Coulson-Thomas, 'Developing Directors, building an effective boardroom team' (McGraw-Hill, 1993)

Differentiation

- Attracting and engaging good customers, business partners and talented people

Colin Coulson-Thomas, 'Shaping Things to Come' (Blackhall Publishing, 2001)

Colin Coulson-Thomas, 'Transforming the Company, manage change, compete and win' (Kogan Page, 2002 & 2004), chapter 4

Colin Coulson-Thomas, 'Individuals and Enterprise, creating entrepreneurs for the new millennium through personal transformation' (Blackhall Publishing, 1999)

Creating New Commercial Offerings

- Challenging assumptions and identifying opportunities
- Creating new options and choices
- Packaging what you know
- Crafting new knowledge-based offerings

Colin Coulson-Thomas, 'Shaping Things to Come, strategies for creating alternative enterprises' (Blackhall Publishing, 2001)

Colin Coulson-Thomas, 'The Knowledge Entrepreneur' (Kogan Page, 2003)

Colin Coulson-Thomas, 'Individuals and Enterprise, creating entrepreneurs for the new millennium through personal transformation' (Blackhall Publishing, 1999)

Business Development

Winning business
* Winning competitive Bids

Pricing for profit
* Justifying a premium price

Building customer relationships
* Strategic and key account management
* Customer service as a business opportunity

Colin Coulson-Thomas, 'Transforming the Company, manage change, compete and win' (Kogan Page, 2002 & 2004), chapters 5 and 6

Colin Coulson-Thomas, Carol Kennedy and Matthew O'Connor, 'Winning New Business, the critical success factors' (Policy Publications, 2002)

Colin Coulson-Thomas, 'Pricing for Profit, the critical success factors' (Policy Publications, 2002)

John Hurcomb [Executive Editor: Colin Coulson-Thomas], 'Developing Strategic Customers & Key Accounts' (Policy Publications, 1998)

Process Improvement, Re-engineering and Transformation

* Opportunity seeking and goal setting
* Selecting the right approach
* Process analysis and redesign
* Implementation and evaluation

Colin Coulson-Thomas, 'The Future of the Organisation, achieving excellence through business transformation' (Kogan Page, 1997 & 1998)

Colin Coulson-Thomas, 'Business Process Re-engineering, Myth & Reality' (Kogan Page, 1994 & 1996)

Colin Coulson-Thomas, 'Transforming the Company, manage change, compete and win' (Kogan Page, 2002 & 2004)

Change Management

- Managing change
- Achieving successful corporate transformation

Colin Coulson-Thomas, 'Transforming the Company, manage change, compete and win' (Kogan Page, 2002 & 2004), chapter 6

Colin Coulson-Thomas, 'The Future of the Organisation, achieving excellence through business transformation' (Kogan Page, 1997 & 1998)

Colin Coulson-Thomas, 'Business Process Re-engineering, Myth & Reality' (Kogan Page, 1994 & 1996)

Corporate Communications

- Effective internal and external communication

Colin Coulson-Thomas, 'Transforming the Company, manage change, compete and win' (Kogan Page, 2002 & 2004), chapter 7

Colin Coulson-Thomas, 'Creating Excellence in the Boardroom, A guide to shaping directorial competence and board effectiveness' (McGraw-Hill, 1993)

New Ways of Working

- Introducing More Flexible Patterns of Work

Colin Coulson-Thomas, 'Transforming the Company, manage change, compete and win' (Kogan Page, 2002 & 2004), chapter 8

Colin Coulson-Thomas [Principal Author], 'The Responsive Organisation, re-engineering new patterns of work' (Policy Publications, 1995)

Corporate Learning

- Integrating learning and working
- Creating a corporate learning strategy

Colin Coulson-Thomas, 'Transforming the Company, manage change, compete and win' (Kogan Page, 2002 & 2004), chapter 17

Colin Coulson-Thomas, 'Developing a Corporate Learning Strategy, the key knowledge management challenge for the HR function' (Policy Publications, 1999).

Knowledge Management and Exploitation

- Knowledge entrepreneurship (making money from what you know)
- Capturing and sharing the expertise of superstars

Colin Coulson-Thomas, 'Transforming the Company, manage change, compete and win' (Kogan Page, 2002 & 2004), chapter 8

Colin Coulson-Thomas, 'The Knowledge Entrepreneur' (Kogan Page, 2003)

Sarah Perrin [Executive Editor: Colin Coulson-Thomas], 'Managing Intellectual Capital to Grow Shareholder Value' (Policy Publications, 2000)

Workgroup Productivity

- Job support tools and increasing key workgroup performance

Colin Coulson-Thomas, 'The Knowledge Entrepreneur' (Kogan Page, 2003)

Quality, Business Excellence and Entrepreneurship

- Creating an entrepreneurial corporate culture

Colin Coulson-Thomas, 'Transforming the Company, manage change, compete and win' (Kogan Page, 2002 & 2004), chapter 9

Colin Coulson-Thomas, 'The Future of the Organisation, achieving excellence through business transformation' (Kogan Page, 1997 & 1998)

Colin Coulson-Thomas, 'Individuals and Enterprise, creating entrepreneurs for the new millennium through personal transformation' (Blackhall Publishing, 1999)

Colin Coulson-Thomas, 'The Knowledge Entrepreneur' (Kogan Page, 2003)

Purchasing

- Entrepreneurial purchasing

Paddy FitzGerald [Executive Editor: Colin Coulson-Thomas], 'Effective Purchasing, the Critical Success Factors' (Policy Publications, 2000)

Operating in the International Marketplace

- Skills and approaches for effective international operation

Colin Coulson-Thomas, 'Transforming the Company, manage change, compete and win' (Kogan Page, 2002 & 2004), chapter 11

Colin Coulson-Thomas, 'Creating the Global Company, successful internationalisation' (McGraw-Hill, 1992)

Collaboration and Partnering

- Building effective business partnerships
- Partnering with customers, suppliers, consultants and business schools

Colin Coulson-Thomas, 'Transforming the Company, manage change, compete and win' (Kogan Page, 2002 & 2004), chapters 12 and 14

John Hurcomb [Executive Editor: Colin Coulson-Thomas], 'Developing Strategic Customers & Key Accounts' (Policy Publications, 1998)

IT and eBusiness

- Getting the infrastructure right
- Supporting the network organisation

Colin Coulson-Thomas, 'Transforming the Company, manage change, compete and win' (Kogan Page, 2002 & 2004), chapter 15

Colin Coulson-Thomas, 'Shaping Things to Come, strategies for creating alternative enterprises' (Blackhall Publishing, 2001)

Next Steps

- Formulating and implementing an action programme

Colin Coulson-Thomas, 'Transforming the Company, manage change, compete and win' (Kogan Page, 2002 & 2004), chapter 18

Masterclass, Seminar or Workshop Leader

Colin Coulson-Thomas, an experienced chairman of award winning companies, the world's first Professor of Corporate Transformation, author of 'Transforming the Company', and an experienced Process Vision Holder of major transformation projects, has reviewed the processes and practices for winning business of over 100 companies, and helped over 100 boards and management teams to improve corporate performance. He can be contacted by tel: + 44 (0)1733 361149; fax: +44 (0)1733 361459 and by email: colinct@tiscali.co.uk or via www.coulson-thomas.com